Project 2000:
Basic

Student Manual

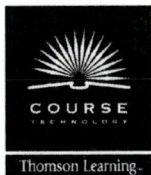

COURSE
TECHNOLOGY

Thomson Learning

Australia • Canada • Mexico • Singapore
Spain • United Kingdom • United States

Project 2000: Basic

VP and GM of Courseware:	Michael Springer
Series Product Managers:	Caryl Bahner-Guhin, Charles G. Blum, and Adam A. Wilcox
Developmental Editor:	Caryl Bahner-Guhin
Production Editor:	Ellina Beletsky
Project Editor:	Cathy Albano
Key Tester:	Bryn Cope
Series Designer:	Adam A. Wilcox
Cover Designer:	Efrat Reis

For more information contact:

Course Technology ILT
One Main Street
Cambridge, MA 02142

Or find us on the Web at: www.course.com

For permission to use material from this text or product, contact us by
• Web: www.thomsonrights.com
• Phone: 1-800-730-2214
• Fax: 1-800-730-2215

Trademarks

Course ILT is a trademark of Course Technology.

Some of the product names and company names used in this book have been used for identification purposes only and may be trademarks or registered trademarks of their respective manufacturers and sellers.

Disclaimer

Course Technology reserves the right to revise this publication and make changes from time to time in its content without notice.

ISBN 0-619-02335-X

Printed in the United States of America

1 2 3 4 5 PM 04 03 02 01

Contents

Project 2000: Basic

Introduction

After reading this introduction, you will know how to:

A Use Course Technology ILT manuals in general.

B Use prerequisites, a target student description, course objectives, and a skills inventory to properly set your expectations for the course.

C Re-key this course after class.

Topic A: About the manual

Course Technology ILT philosophy

Course Technology ILT manuals facilitate your learning by providing structured interaction with the software itself. While we provide text to explain difficult concepts, the hands-on activities are the focus of our courses. By paying close attention as your instructor leads you through these activities, you will learn the skills and concepts effectively.

We believe strongly in the instructor-led classroom. During class, focus on your instructor. Our manuals are designed and written to facilitate your interaction with your instructor, and not to call attention to manuals themselves.

We believe in the basic approach of setting expectations, delivering instruction, and providing summary and review afterwards. For this reason, lessons begin with objectives and end with summaries. We also provide overall course objectives and a course summary to provide both an introduction to and closure on the entire course.

Manual components

The manuals contain these major components:

1 Table of contents
2 Introduction
3 Units
4 Course summary
5 Reference
6 Index

Each element is described below.

Table of contents

The table of contents acts as a learning roadmap.

Introduction

The introduction contains information about our training philosophy and our manual components, features, and conventions. It contains target student, prerequisite, objective, and setup information for the specific course.

Units

Units are the largest structural component of the course content. A unit begins with a title page that lists objectives for each major subdivision, or topic, within the unit. Within each topic, conceptual and explanatory information alternates with hands-on activities. Units conclude with a summary comprising one paragraph for each topic, and an independent practice activity that gives you an opportunity to practice the skills you've learned.

The conceptual information takes the form of text paragraphs, exhibits, lists, and tables. The activities are structured in two columns, one telling you what to do, the other providing explanations, descriptions, and graphics.

Course summary

This section provides a text summary of the entire course. It is useful for providing closure at the end of the course. The course summary also indicates the next course in this series, if there is one, and lists additional resources you might find useful as you continue to learn about the software.

Reference

The reference is an at-a-glance job aid summarizing some of the more common features of the software.

Index

The index enables you to quickly find information about a particular feature or concept of the software.

Manual conventions

We've tried to keep the number of elements and the types of formatting to a minimum in the manuals. This aids in clarity and makes the manuals more classically elegant looking. But there are some conventions and icons you should know about.

Convention/Icon	Description
Italic text	In conceptual text, indicates a new term or feature.
Bold text	In unit summaries, indicates a key term or concept. In an independent practice activity, indicates an explicit item that you select, choose, or type.
Code font	Indicates code or syntax.
Select **bold item**	In the left column of hands-on activities, bold sans-serif text indicates an explicit item that you select, choose, or type.
Keycaps like [↵ ENTER]	Indicate a key on the keyboard you must press.

Hands-on activities

The hands-on activities are the most important parts of our manuals. They are divided into two primary columns. The "Here's how" column gives short instructions to you about what to do. The "Here's why" column provides explanations, graphics, and clarifications. Here's a sample:

Do it!

A-1:   Activity Title

Here's how	Here's why
1 Open **Sales**	This is an oversimplified sales compensation worksheet. It shows sales totals, commissions, and incentives for 5 sales reps.
2 Observe the contents of cell F4	F4 ▼ =E4*C_Rate The commission rate formulas use the name "C_Rate" instead of a value for the commission rate.

Topic B: Setting your expectations

Properly setting your expectations is essential to your success. This topic will help you do that by providing:

- Prerequisites for this course
- A description of the target student at whom the course is aimed
- A list of the objectives for the course
- A skills assessment for the course

Course prerequisites

Before taking this course, you should be familiar with personal computers and the use of a keyboard and a mouse. Furthermore, this course assumes that you've completed the following courses or have equivalent experience:

- *Windows 95: Module 1* or *Windows 98: Module 1*

Target student

The target students for this course should be comfortable using a personal computer and Microsoft Windows 95 or later. Students should know the basics of project management techniques. Students will get most out of this course if their goal is to become proficient managers by using Microsoft Project 2000 to create efficient and cost-effective projects for their organizations.

Course objectives

These overall course objectives will give you an idea about what to expect from the course. It is also possible that they will help you see that this course is not the right one for you. If you think you either lack the prerequisite knowledge or already know most of the subject matter to be covered, you should let your instructor know that you think you are misplaced in the class.

After completing this course, you will know how to:

- Apply project management concepts, start Microsoft Project 2000, open an existing file, use the Office Assistant, create, save, and close a new project file, and exit Microsoft Project 2000.

- Create a task list, modify the task list, create the Work Breakdown Structure (WBS), and view, define and apply WBS codes.

- Create task links, and add lead time, explore Network Diagram view, modify task links, add advanced task information.

- Use the Change Working Time dialog box to create a new base calendar, task calendar and resource calendar, use Resource Sheet view to enter resource information, assign resources to tasks, and work with resource costs.

- Examine and customize Calendar view, and customize Gantt Chart and Network Diagram view.
- Edit task constraints, edit an effort-driven schedule, and identify and resolve resource overallocation.
- Use standard filters and AutoFilters to view data, create a custom filter, use predefined groups, and create a custom group, and sort tasks and resources.

Skills inventory

Use the following form to gauge your skill level entering the class. For each skill listed, rate your familiarity from 1 to 5, with five being the most familiar. *This is not a test.* Rather, it is intended to provide you with an idea of where you're starting from at the beginning of class. If you're wholly unfamiliar with all the skills, you might not be ready for the class. If you think you already understand all of the skills, you might need to move on to the next Module in the series. In either case, you should let your instructor know as soon as possible.

Skill	1	2	3	4	5
Apply project management concepts					
Start Microsoft Project 2000					
Open an existing project file					
Navigating different views of Project 2000					
Create a project file					
Set the project's start date					
Save and close a project file					
Exit Microsoft Project 2000					
Create and modify a task list					
Create the Work Breakdown Structure					
View, define, and apply WBS codes					
Link and unlink tasks					
Add lead time between tasks					
Explore and modify task links in Network Diagram view					
Insert a task type					
Set up milestone tasks					

Skill	1	2	3	4	5
Define a task constraint					
Create a base calendar					
Create and apply a task calendar					
Create a resource pool and a resource calendar					
Assign resources to tasks					
Work with resource costs					
Explore and customize Calendar view					
Customize Gantt Chart view and Network Diagram view					
Edit task constraints					
Edit effort-driven schedules					
Identify and resolve resource overallocation					
Use standard filters and AutoFilters					
Use predefined groups and create a custom group					
Sort tasks and resources					

Topic C: Re-keying the course

If you have the proper hardware and software, you can re-key this course after class. This section explains what you'll need in order to do so, and how to do it.

Computer requirements

To re-key this course, your personal computer must have:

- A keyboard and a mouse
- A Pentium 75 MHz processor or higher
- A minimum of 16 MB RAM for Windows 95 machines and a minimum of 32 MB RAM for Windows NT machines
- 30 MB of available hard disk space for typical installation
- A printer driver installed, or you will not be able to view the pagination while zooming in and out of Network Diagram view
- CD-ROM drive and 3 ½ inch floppy disk drive if you want to load the data from the disk
- VGA or higher resolution monitor
- Internet access if you will be downloading data files from www.courseilt.com

Setup instructions to re-key the course

Before you re-key the course, you will need to perform the following steps.

1   If necessary, reset any defaults that you have changed. If you do not wish to reset the defaults, you can still re-key the course, but some activities might not work exactly as documented.
2   Create a folder called Student Data at the root of the hard drive.
3   Download the Student Data examples for the course (if you do not have an Internet connection, you can ask your instructor for a copy of the data files on a diskette).
   1   Connect to www.courseilt.com.
   2   Click the download link for the Student Data folder.
   3   To save the data files, follow the instructions that appear on your screen.
4   Copy the data files for the course to the Student Data folder.

Unit 1

Project 2000 basics

Complete this unit, and you'll know how to:

A Apply project management concepts.

B Start Project 2000, open an existing project file, and navigate different views.

C Use the Office Assistant to access information.

D Create and save a new project file.

E Close a project file and exit Project 2000.

Topic A: Project management concepts

Explanation

As a project manager, you are required to manage and control your project to make it a success. To do this, you need to know project management concepts and be able to apply them. You can use the tools of Project 2000 to handle your project effectively.

Features of a successful project

A *project* can be defined as a one-time, organized effort toward a specific goal. Every project must have a definite start and end. Its distinctive characteristic is that it creates a unique product or service. Projects are often the critical components of the performing organization's business strategy and link to the ongoing operations of the organization.

A project has three specific components:

- Objectives - the customer requirements, quality specifications, deliverable
- Budget - cost, resources
- Schedule - time lines for different tasks, specific start and end dates

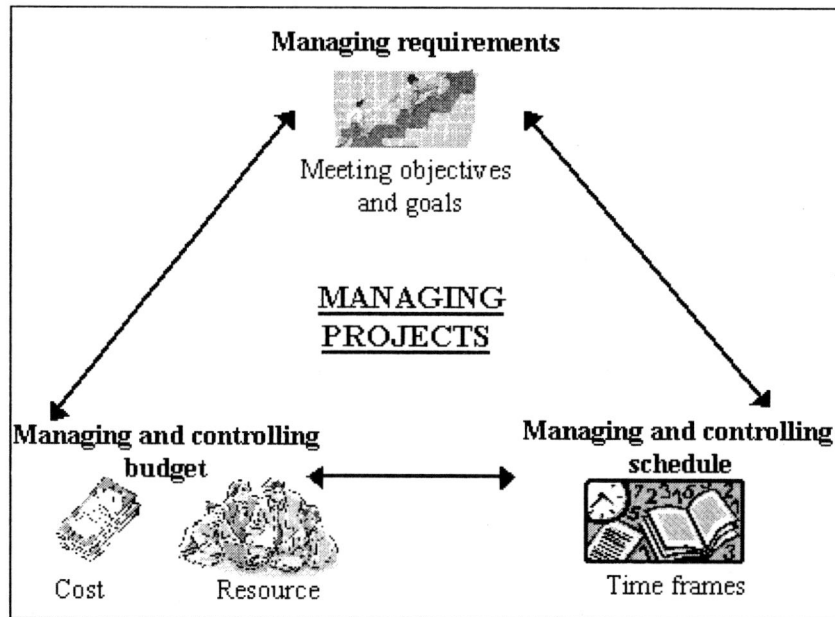

Exhibit 1-1: The components of a project

A project is considered to be successful when it is delivered on time, within budget, and meets the customer requirements.

To manage your project well, you break the project into phases so that they are easily controlled. The four phases are the initial phase, planning phase, implementation phase, and close out phase. Collectively, these phases comprise the project life cycle. Each phase is marked by the completion of one or more deliverables and these deliverables are called *milestones*.

Project management

Project management is the application of knowledge, skills, tools, and techniques to accomplish activities or tasks to meet the objectives set for a project. To manage the project, you need to understand the basic processes involved in project management. The project management process consists of defining the priorities, limitations, and constraints for the project. It focuses on describing and organizing the work of the project. Exhibit 1-2 shows the link between the process groups in a life cycle of a project.

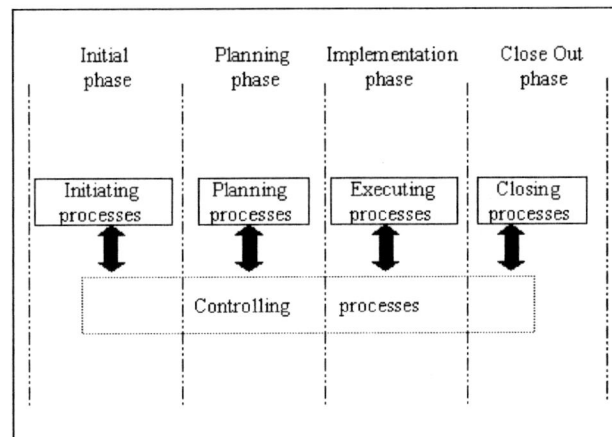

Exhibit 1-2: The links between process groups

The project management processes can be grouped into the following:

- Initiating processes recognize the beginning of the project.

- Planning processes devise and maintain a workable scheme to meet the objectives and business needs of the project. They identify the scope of the project, and the tasks and their resource requirements.

- Executing processes coordinate people and other resources to carry out the plan by assigning tasks to the right people, setting up deadlines, and deciding the right sequence of activities.

- Controlling processes ensure that the objectives are met by monitoring and tracking the project's progress. Monitoring involves reviewing the progress of the project against the plan, and leads to control measures being taken. *Control* means taking corrective measures to ensure the success of the project.

- Closing processes formalize acceptance of the project and ensure an orderly end.

For smooth progress of the project, you need to track and control the project. Here, you have to consider the constraints that the project might face. *Constraints* are the limitations imposed on your project. There can be financial or resource constraints. You can handle constraints by trying to minimize risk, cost, and resources in an effective manner. However, the main constraint that affects the performance of a project is time. You can manage your project well if you allocate proper time frames for each project phase.

Do it!

A-1:   Discussing project management concepts

Question	Answer
1 What is a project?	
2 Would you consider 'Launching a new product' as a project and why?	
3 Why is planning necessary for a project?	
4 Why do you need to monitor your project?	
5 When launching a new product, you are asked to complete the campaign in 5 days. In your opinion, you need at least 12 days for the task. What type of constraint do you face?	

Introduction to Project 2000

Explanation

Managing a large project can become very difficult if it is not planned well. A project can fail if the time to execute it exceeds the planned duration, the cost of it exceeds the planned budget, or the end deliverable, or product, does not meet the specifications. To handle your project effectively and efficiently, a project management application such as Project 2000 is very useful. By using Project 2000, you can effectively organize, schedule, manage, and report your project.

Exhibit 1-3 displays the tasks that can be accomplished by using Project 2000.

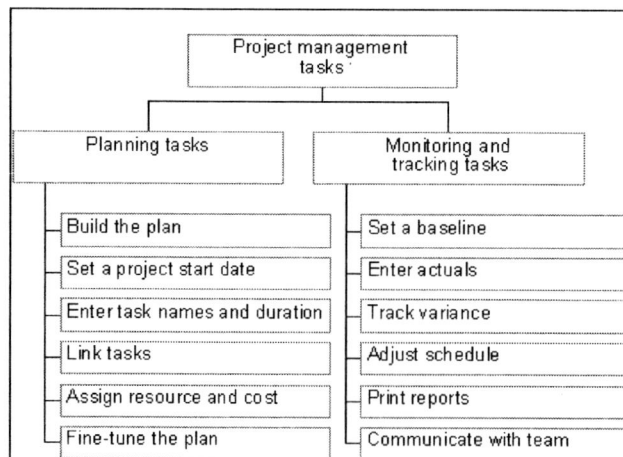

```
                    ┌──────────────────────┐
                    │  Project management  │
                    │        tasks         │
                    └──────────┬───────────┘
              ┌────────────────┴────────────────┐
     ┌────────┴─────────┐           ┌────────────┴──────────┐
     │  Planning tasks  │           │  Monitoring and       │
     │                  │           │  tracking tasks       │
     └────────┬─────────┘           └────────────┬──────────┘
     ├─ Build the plan              ├─ Set a baseline
     ├─ Set a project start date    ├─ Enter actuals
     ├─ Enter task names and duration ├─ Track variance
     ├─ Link tasks                  ├─ Adjust schedule
     ├─ Assign resource and cost    ├─ Print reports
     └─ Fine-tune the plan          └─ Communicate with team
```

Exhibit 1-3: The basic tasks that can be done with Project 2000

Tools of Project 2000

When you create a project plan, you list tasks and subtasks in Gantt Chart view. The Gantt chart is one of the tools that is commonly used to enter task-related information. Project 2000 has a built-in feature that helps you create the Work Breakdown Structure. The Work Breakdown Structure is a hierarchical structure that allows you to list the tasks at their lowest level. After you identify the tasks and the relationships between them, you create task dependencies. Project 2000 automatically schedules the tasks to start and finish based on their relationship with each other.

The Network Diagram view displays the project details as a drawing that shows how tasks are arranged, helping you to visualize and analyze task relationships.

You can use the Calendar view to display your project dates chronologically. You can also use this tool to evaluate the effort in calendar days.

Several tools provided by Project 2000 enable you to work with resource assignment, cost, overallocation, and leveling. You enter resource information in the resource sheet. Project 2000 automatically calculates the total cost for the resources based on the values that you enter. After entering resource information, you can estimate resource utilization by using Resource Usage view. Project 2000 also allows you to identify resource allocation. By using the Resource Graph, you can identify the allocation of work or cost of resources over a specific time frame.

The Variance table is a tool that tracks the variance of costs. *Variance* is the difference between the actual and the planned costs. Project 2000 also allows you to import and export data from other applications such as Microsoft Excel. In addition, you can export project data to the Web and insert hyperlinks to tasks and resources. With Project Central, you can communicate project details to your team. You can also use email and the Web as the messaging methods to communicate project information.

Do it!

A-2:   Matching management concepts and tools

Question	Answer
1 What is a Gantt chart?	
2 What is a Work Breakdown Structure?	
3 What is a network diagram?	
4 How does a Calendar view help in project management?	
5 Which tools help you manage your resources?	

Topic B: Exploring the Project 2000 window

Explanation

Project 2000 has an intuitive, user-friendly interface. The menu commands and the toolbar buttons enable you to access commands and functions. You begin a project by specifying the start date for the project. Project 2000 automatically organizes all the tasks as scheduled work according to calendar dates, and schedules the first task from the start date of the project.

Getting started with Project 2000

After you have planned the basic tasks to accomplish your project, you can start working with Project 2000. The simplest way that you can start Project 2000 is by clicking the Start button, and then choosing Programs, Microsoft Project. When you open Project 2000, a new project file called "Project1" appears in the Microsoft Project window along with a Microsoft Project Help window. The screen displays five types of learning aids. You can go through Project 2000 tutorials, watch a preview, learn what's new in Project 2000, use the Office Assistant and references, or navigate the pre-designed map to start working with Project 2000.

Components of the Microsoft Project 2000 window

The Microsoft Project 2000 window has many components through which you can interact and get information about what you are working on. Exhibit 1-4 shows some of these components.

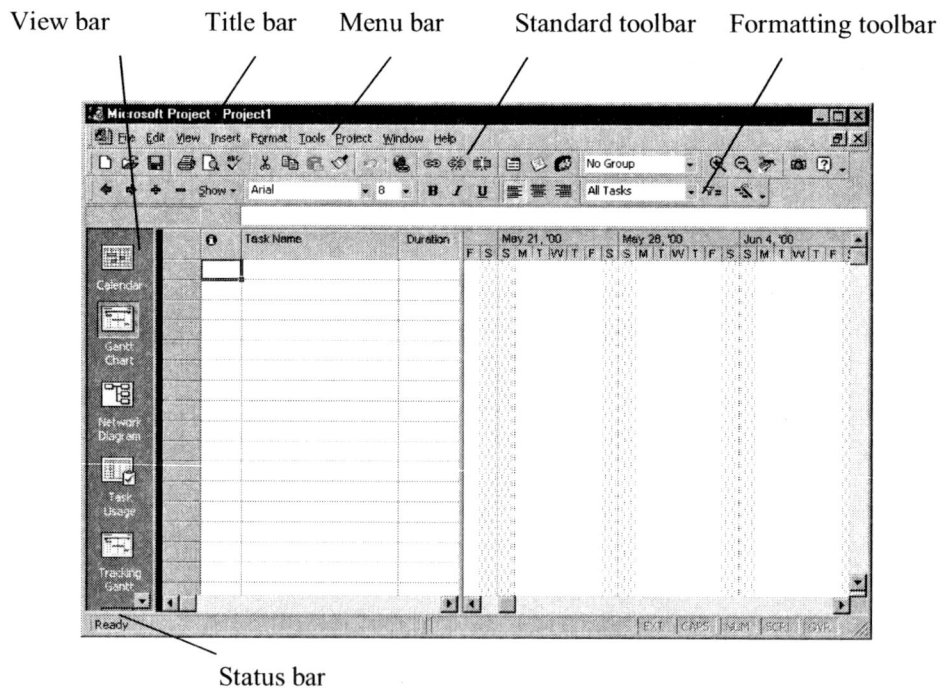

Exhibit 1-4: The default Microsoft Project 2000 window

The following table explains the components of the Microsoft Project 2000 window.

Component	Description
Title bar	It displays the name of the project file. The default name provided by Project 2000 for the first project you open is "Project1."
Menu bar	It displays all menus that are available in Project 2000. Each menu consists of a set of commands.
Standard toolbar	It contains buttons for frequently used commands, such as Open or Save. The buttons are shortcuts to the menu commands.
Formatting toolbar	It contains buttons for formatting and outlining text. The buttons are shortcuts to the menu commands.
View bar	It contains buttons used to switch to different Project 2000 views.
Status bar	It displays the information about a selected command or an operation in progress. It is located at the bottom of the window and displays the current status of the project file.

Do it!

B-1: Starting Project 2000

Here's how	Here's why
1 Choose **Start**, **Programs**, **Microsoft Project**	To start Project 2000.
2 Observe the Microsoft Project Help window	
3 Click ▣	To maximize the Microsoft Project Help window. You can go through Project 2000 tutorials, watch a preview, find out what's new in Microsoft Project 2000, use the Office Assistant and references, or navigate the pre-designed map to work with Project 2000.
Click ☒	(The Close button is on the upper-right corner of the Microsoft Project Help window.) To close the window.

4 Observe the title bar	**Microsoft Project - Project1**
	It shows the name of the program, "Microsoft Project," and the name of the current project, "Project1."
5 Observe the menu bar	It contains the menus that are available in Project 2000.
6 Observe the toolbars	The Standard and Formatting toolbars appear by default. They have buttons that help you to perform common tasks quickly.
7 Point to the button on the Standard toolbar, as shown	
	A ToolTip appears below the button, specifying the name of the button.
8 Observe the View bar	It contains the different view options.
9 Observe the Status bar	It shows the current state of the window.

Opening a Project 2000 file

Explanation

You can open an existing Project 2000 file to view the task list and start working with it. Project 2000 opens the project file in the default Gantt Chart view. To open an existing file:

1 Choose File, Open to display the Open dialog box.
2 Select the folder and file name of the project file that you want to open.
3 Click Open.

Examining Gantt Chart view

Gantt Chart view is the default view of Project 2000. It is divided into two panes. The left pane is called the Gantt table, which is like a spreadsheet with rows, columns, and cells. You can insert task names in the cells under the respective column headings. Each column displays information that is stored in the Microsoft Project database. The row numbers are the ID for each task.

The right pane is called the Gantt chart. It displays the information on the left in a graphic representation. Gantt Chart view displays the default timescale that shows the month and days on a weekly basis. Bars represent the tasks and the length of the bar depicts the duration of each task. You can also compare the start and finish dates of the task by viewing the length of the task bar.

You can use the horizontal and vertical scroll bars on each pane to view the other columns and to move forward in the timescale.

Indicators field   Column heading   Gantt table pane   Timescale

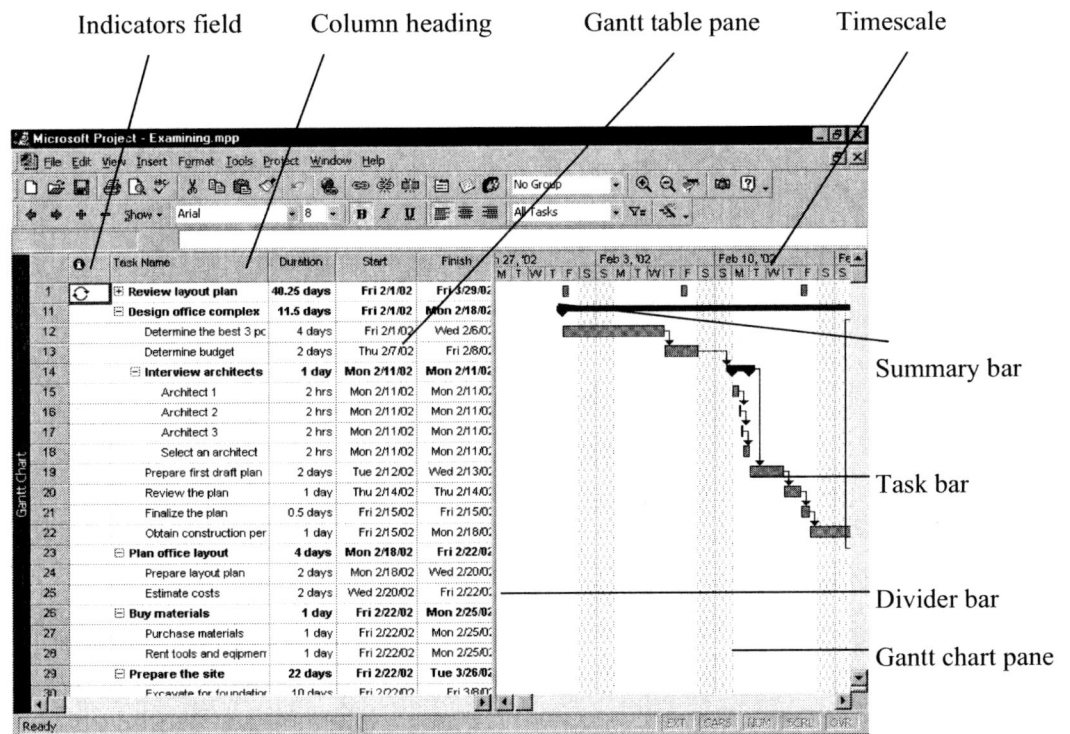

Exhibit 1-5: A sample project file in Gantt Chart view

Do it!

B-2: Opening an existing project in Gantt Chart view

Here's how	Here's why
1 Choose **File, Open...**	To display the Open dialog box.
2 From the Look in list, select **Student Data**	You'll select a file from this folder.
Select **Examining.mpp**	You'll use this file to examine the different views in Project 2000.
3 Click **Open**	To open the file in Gantt Chart view.
4 Choose **View**, **View Bar**	To hide the View bar.
Observe Gantt Chart view	The View bar is hidden and a label, "Gantt Chart," appears.
5 Observe the left pane	The Gantt table displays the list of tasks in a project. Each row represents a task and the row numbers represent the task ID.

Summary bar

Task bar

Divider bar

Gantt chart pane

6	Observe the column headings	By default, Project 2000 provides the headings. Each column displays information from the Project 2000 database.
	Scroll horizontally	(On the left pane.) To view the other column headings.
7	Observe the Indicators field	It displays icons, which indicate task-related information.
8	Point as shown	

Start	Finish	h 27, '02							Feb 3
		M	T	W	T	F	S	S	M
Fri 2/1/02	**Fri 3/29/02**						▯		
Fri 2/1/02	**Mon 2/18/02**						▼		
Fri 2/1/02	Wed 2/6/02						▓▓▓		

The pointer changes to a double-headed arrow when positioned on the divider bar. You can drag it either way to change the width of a pane.

9	Observe the right pane	The Gantt chart displays the left side information in a graphical form.
10	Observe the timescale	It shows the months and the days of the week.
11	Observe the task bars	The length of each task bar depicts the duration of the tasks. You can see the start and end dates for each task.

Exploring other views

Explanation

Project 2000 provides several views that allow you to work with the project data in different formats or views. The View bar displays buttons of the most commonly used views.

The following table describes the views on the View bar.

Icon	View	Use
	Calendar	To show the tasks that are scheduled over a specific week or range of weeks.
	Gantt Chart	To enter and schedule a task list.
	Network Diagram	To create a flowchart format for the scheduled task list.
	Task Usage	To see the resources that are assigned to the tasks.

Icon	View	Use
	Tracking Gantt	To compare the baseline with the actual schedule.
	Resource Graph	To show the information regarding a single resource or a group of resources.
	Resource Sheet	To enter resource information in a spreadsheet-like format.
	Resource Usage	To show the cost, work, or overallocation for each resource.

Do it!

B-3: Navigating views

Here's how	Here's why
1 Choose **View**, **View Bar**	To show the View bar.
Click	(The Down arrow button on the View bar.) To scroll down the View bar to see the other view buttons.
Click	(The Up arrow button on the View bar.) To scroll up the View bar.
2 Click	(The Calendar button is on the View bar.) To switch to Calendar view.
3 Observe the view	The tasks span across dates in the calendar according to their duration.
4 Click	(The Network Diagram button is on the View bar.) To switch to Network Diagram view.
5 Observe Network Diagram view	The boxes represent the tasks and the lines show that the tasks are linked.

Topic C: Using Help

Explanation

You can use Project's Help system to get assistance while you are working. You can access Help by choosing Help, Microsoft Project Help, by pressing F1 on the keyboard, or by using the Office Assistant. You can also get help from Microsoft through the Web.

The Office Assistant

Project 2000 provides the Office Assistant, which facilitates easy access to the Help feature of Project 2000. The Office Assistant is an animated Help system that can answer your questions while you work. The Assistant lets you type questions in plain language and then displays relevant help topics. To show the Office Assistant, choose Help, Microsoft Project Help or click the Office Assistant button on the Standard toolbar. You can also hide the Office Assistant by choosing Help, Hide Office Assistant, or by right-clicking on it and choosing Hide.

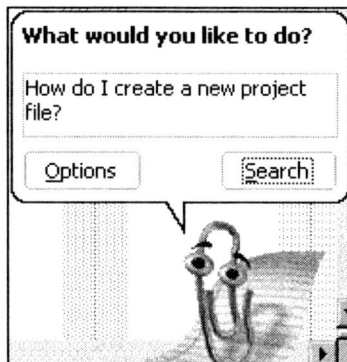

Exhibit 1-6: The Office Assistant

To find help in Project 2000, open the Office Assistant, type a few words in the balloon about what you want to do, and click Search.

Do it!   **C-1:   Using the Office Assistant**

Here's how	Here's why
1 Choose **Help, Microsoft Project Help**	The Office Assistant appears, prompting you to type in your question.
2 Edit the What would you like to do box to read **How do I create a new project file?**	To search for an answer to this question.
3 Click **Search**	To display a list of related options.
4 Click **Start a new file**	To display the Help topic.
Observe the screen	The Microsoft Project Help window appears.
5 Observe the Microsoft Project Help window	Information on creating a new Project file and related information appears.
6 Click ⊠	(The Close button is on the upper-right corner of the Microsoft Project Help window.) To close the Help window.
7 Choose **Help, Hide the Office Assistant**	To hide the Office Assistant.

Topic D: Working with a project file

Explanation

After starting Project 2000, you create a new project file to begin working with your project. In the Initial phase of your project, you need to plan and organize your project. You start by setting the start or finish date for your project. Then, you save the project file so that you can use it later.

Starting a project

When you start Project 2000, by default, a new project file appears in Gantt Chart view. You can start working with this default project file, create a new blank project file, create a customized project file by using templates, or open an existing project file. *Templates* are predefined formats that Project 2000 provides to create projects according to your needs.

You create a new blank project file by choosing File, New. The New dialog box appears. By default, the General tab is active and the Blank Project template is selected. You can also click the New button in the Standard toolbar to create a new project file.

Using the Project Information dialog box

When you create a new blank project file, Project 2000 displays the Project Information dialog box. Exhibit 1-7 shows the Project Information for 'Project2' dialog box. The Project Information dialog box contains essential information for efficient project management. The Schedule from list provides two options: Project Start Date and Project Finish Date. Exhibit 1-7 shows the Schedule from option with Project Start Date selected. You can set either the start date or the finish date for your project. If you know the start date for your project and want Project 2000 to schedule your project accordingly, select Project Start Date. Project 2000 schedules your project to begin as soon as possible from the specified start date after considering factors like default non-working time and holidays.

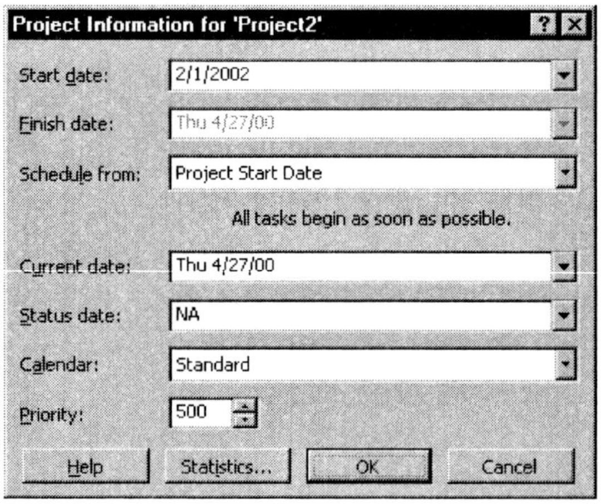

Exhibit 1-7: A sample Project Information dialog box

Using the Project Properties dialog box

You use the Properties dialog box to enter information about the project, such as the title of the project, author, the manager's name, and the name of your company. With this information, you can locate your project file easily. For example, if you want to locate the project file handled by a specific manager, you can use the Tools option in the Open dialog box to find any project files that have that manager's name in the properties.

You can open the Properties dialog box by choosing File, Properties.

Do it!

D-1:   Creating a new project file

Here's how	Here's why
1 Choose **File, New...**	To open the New dialog box.
2 Click **OK**	This will create a new blank project file. You can also click the New button in the Standard toolbar to create a new blank project file.
3 Observe the title bar	By default, Project 2000 assigns the name "Project2" to the new project file.
4 Observe the dialog box	The Project Information dialog box appears and displays the current date as the project start date.
5 In the Start date box, enter **2/1/2002**	This will be the start date of the project.
6 In the Schedule from list, verify that Project Start Date is selected	To specify that the date you enter is the project's start date.
7 Click **OK**	To close the dialog box.
8 Choose **File, Properties**	To open the Properties dialog box.
9 Verify that the Summary tab is active	You'll enter information in the different options provided in it.

10 Edit the Title box to read
    **Building a new office
    complex**

    This will be the title of the project.

    Edit the other boxes to read as
    shown

General	Summary	Statistics	Contents	Custom

Title: | Building a new office complex

Subject: |

Author: | Kathy Sinclair

Manager: | Kathy Sincalir

Company: | Outlander Spices

11 Click **OK**

    To close the dialog box.

Saving a project file

Explanation

After you have created a project file and specified a start date for your project, you need to save the project file to preserve the information for future use. The first time you save a project file, you specify a file name and location. In the future, you can save the document again with the same name, or with a different name in a different location.

To save a project file for the first time:

1 Choose File, Save As to open the Save As dialog box (as shown in Exhibit 1-8).
2 From the Save in list, select a directory or a folder where you want to store the project file.
3 In the File name box, specify the project file name.
4 Click Save.

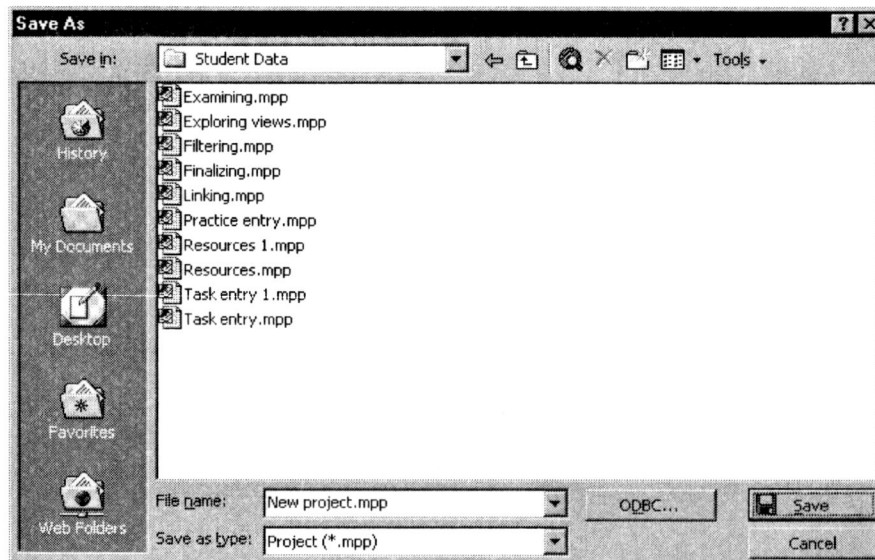

Exhibit 1-8: A sample Save As dialog box

Do it!

D-2:   Saving a project file

Here's how	Here's why
1 Choose **File, Save As...**	To save the project file.
2 Observe the dialog box	The Save As dialog box saves project files in the specified folder.
3 From the Save in list, select **Student Data**	(If necessary.) You'll save the project file in this folder.
4 Observe the File name box	By default, Project 2000 specifies Project2 as the file name.
5 Edit the File name box to read **New project.mpp**	(As shown in Exhibit 1-8.) This will be the project file name.
6 In the Save as type list, verify that Project (*.mpp) is selected	Project 2000 saves project files with an .mpp extension.
7 Click **Save**	To save the file in the specified folder.
8 Observe the title bar	🗗 **Microsoft Project - New project.mpp**
	The title bar automatically updates to show the name of the current project file.

Setting a default folder and Auto Save

Explanation

You may lose any changes you have made to a project file since you last saved it due to power failures and other interruptions. Project 2000 provides an automatic save feature that you can set to ensure that your documents are saved regularly. This feature is called *Auto Save,* and is found under the Save tab in the Options dialog box. Here you can specify the number of minutes that Project 2000 will wait before automatically saving your work. Project 2000 also allows you to specify a folder in which Project will save your project files by default. You can specify this default folder by modifying the File Locations option under the Save tab.

To set a default folder and Auto Save:

1   Choose Tools, Options.
2   Click the Save tab.
3   Under File Locations, in the File types list, verify that Projects is selected.
4   Click Modify to open the Modify Location dialog box.
5   From the Look in list, select the folder that you want.
6   Click OK to close the Modify Location dialog box.
7   Under Auto Save, check Save every.
8   In the minutes spinner box, enter the number of minutes that you want.
9   Click OK to close the Options dialog box.

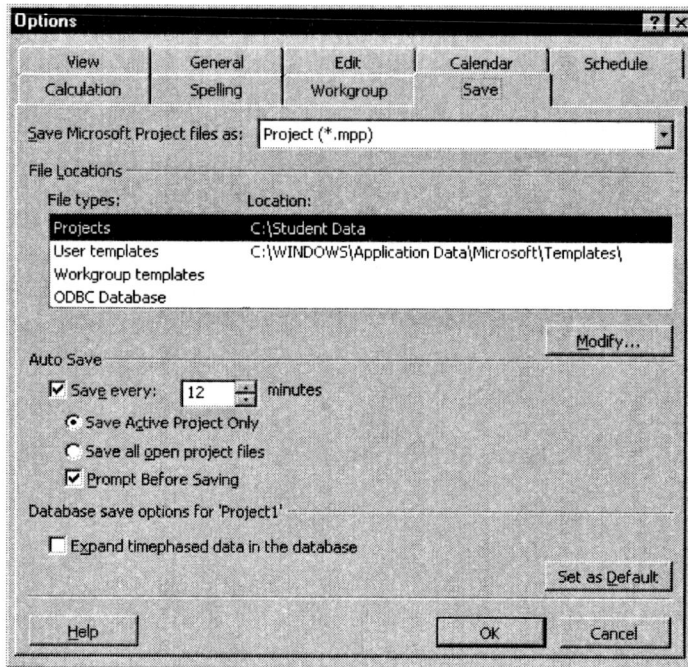

Exhibit 1-9: The Save tab of the Options dialog box

Do it!

D-3:   Setting Auto Save

Here's how	Here's why
1 Choose **Tools, Options...**	To open the Options dialog box.
2 Click the **Save** tab	To view the Save options.
3 Under File Locations, in the File types list, verify that Projects is selected.	You'll modify the default file location of the project files.
4 Click **Modify**	To open the Modify Location dialog box.
5 From the Look in list, select **Student Data**	To set Student Data as the default folder to save the project files.
6 Click **OK**	To close the Modify Location dialog box.

7	Under Auto Save, check **Save every**	To specify the duration of Auto Save.
	In the minutes spinner box, enter **12**	Project 2000 will automatically save the project file after every 12 minutes.
	Verify that Save Active Project Only is selected	By default, Project 2000 saves only the currently active project file.
8	Click **Cancel**	To close the Options dialog box.

Topic E: Closing a project file and exiting Project 2000

Explanation

After you have finished working with your project file, you'll close it and exit Project 2000.

Closing a project file

You can close a file by choosing File, Close or by clicking the Close button in the upper-right corner of the window. You'll see that a warning box appears that prompts you to save any changes made to the existing project file.

Exiting Project 2000

You can exit Project 2000 by choosing File, Exit or by clicking the Close button on the upper-right corner of the Microsoft Project window.

Do it!

E-1: Closing a file and exiting Project 2000

Here's how	Here's why
1 Choose **File, Close**	To close the "New project" project file.
2 Choose **File, Close**	To close the "Examining.mpp" project file. A warning message appears.
3 Click **No**	

To close the file without saving.

4 Choose **File, Exit**	To exit Project 2000.

Unit Summary: Project 2000 basics

Topic A   In this Unit, you learned the **concepts** of **project management**. You learned about the basic tasks required to plan a project, and how **Project 2000** helps you to manage your project in an effective and efficient manner.

Topic B   Then, you learned to **start** Project 2000 and **open** an existing file. You used the existing file to **navigate** different views in Project 2000.

Topic C   Next, you learned to use **Office Assistant** to access the Help feature of Project 2000 by using the **Help** menu commands.

Topic D   Then, you learned to create a **new** project file and use the **Project Information** dialog box to set the start date for the project. You used the **Properties** dialog box to enter project information. You also learned to **save** the project file by using the **Save As** command and to save project files automatically by using the **Auto Save** feature.

Topic E   Finally, you learned to **close** the active project file and **exit** Project 2000 by using the File menu commands.

Independent practice activity

1   Start Project 2000.

2   Close the Microsoft Project Help window.

3   Create a new project file.

4   Set the start date as **10/1/2002**.

5   Schedule the project to begin from the specified start date.

6   Specify the project properties as shown in Exhibit 1-10. (Choose File, Properties.)

7   Open the Save As dialog box.

8   In the Student Data folder, save the Project file as **My practice project**.

9   Close My practice project.

General	Summary	Statistics	Contents	Custom
Title:	Launch of new product line			
Subject:				
Author:	Ann Salinski			
Manager:	Ann Salinski			
Company:	Outlander Spices			

Exhibit 1-10: The Project Properties dialog box after Step 6 of the Independent practice activity

Unit 2

Working with tasks

Complete this unit, and you'll know how to:

A Create a task list in Gantt Chart view by entering the task name and duration.

B Modify the task list by inserting and deleting tasks.

C Create the Work Breakdown Structure by indenting and outdenting tasks.

D View, define, and apply WBS codes.

Topic A: Creating a task list

Explanation

You perform many activities when working on a project. When you use Project 2000, each activity in your project is a task. You begin your project planning by listing the major phases as tasks, and then identify the subtasks for each phase. After you finish identifying all tasks for your project, you estimate the time needed to accomplish each task. Then, you organize the tasks so that you can create a hierarchical structure to identify the occurrence of each task.

Entering tasks

You create a task list by entering all the tasks that must be accomplished in order to complete the project. This helps you determine what resources and time you'll need to complete the project. For example, when your project is to build an office complex, one major phase is construction. Subtasks under construction might include leveling the land and building the foundation.

The information regarding the tasks constitutes a *task list*. A task list is a complete list of tasks and subtasks. You enter information on tasks as rows in the Gantt table, and list them in their order of occurrence.

Task durations

After you've identified and listed all the tasks, you need to plan the time frames for each task so that you can allocate time for each of them. You specify the duration or time needed to complete a task by entering the information in the Gantt table. By default, Project 2000 allocates an *estimated duration* of one day for each task. A question mark after the duration indicates an estimate. You can change an estimated duration to an accurate one. When a cell in the Duration field is selected, it changes to a spinner box. You can use the Up Arrow to increase the duration and the Down Arrow to decrease the duration. To specify the duration in hours, you have to select the cell in the Duration field and enter its value. A horizontal bar shows the time needed for each task in the Gantt chart.

The Planning Wizard

The *Planning Wizard* is a tool provided by Project 2000 to monitor your project. The Planning Wizard appears whenever it identifies information that might cause a conflict such as resource mishandling or other issues that affect the project schedule. The Wizard also provides solutions to the problems and prompts you to take proper action.

When you save the file, the Planning Wizard prompts you to save the file with or without a *baseline*. A baseline is the original plan that you enter for your project. It is used to track the progress of the project.

Do it!

A-1: Adding tasks and durations

Here's how	Here's why
1 Open Task entry	(Choose File, Open.) You'll enter the task list and durations.
2 Choose **Project, Project Information...**	To open the Project Information dialog box.
In the Start date box, verify that 2/1/02 is selected	To confirm the start date for the project.
Click **OK**	To close the dialog box.
3 In the Task Name field, select the first cell	You'll enter the first task.
4 Enter **Design office complex**	This is the first task of the project.
Press TAB	To move to the Duration field. The cell changes to a spinner box.
Observe the selected cell	`1 day? ⬍`
	1day? appears by default. A question mark after the duration value indicates an estimated duration.
5 In the Duration field, enter **2**	This value is the task's duration, in days.
Press ↵ ENTER	To deselect the cell.
Observe the duration field of task 1	`2 days`
	The duration value does not have a question mark after it, and the value changes from estimated to accurate.
6 In the Task Name field, select the second cell	
Enter **Determine the best 3 potential architects**	This is the second task of the project.

7	In the Duration field, enter **4**	This is the task's duration, in days.
	Deselect the cell	Click any other cell.
	Observe the Gantt chart	

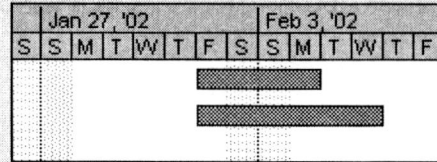

The task bar expands to indicate the task duration.

8	Enter other task details as shown	

9	Choose **File, Save As...**	To save the project file with a new name. The Save As dialog box appears.
	In the Save in list, verify that Student Data is selected	To save the project file in this folder.
	Edit the File name box to read **My task entry**	This is the new project file name.
10	Click **Save**	To save the project file. The Planning Wizard dialog box appears.
	Click **OK**	

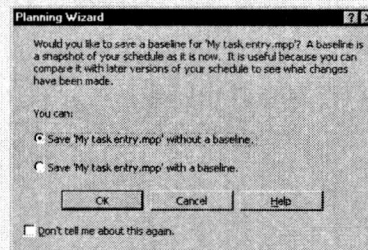

To save the project without a baseline. A baseline is the original plan for your project.

11	Close the project file	Choose File, Close.

Topic B: Modifying a task list

Explanation

During the project cycle, you might encounter a situation in which you have to add or delete planned tasks. You might also need to move tasks to rearrange them in the project.

Inserting tasks

As you plan the task list, you might need to add some tasks to the project. For example, to select an architect for the project, you have to schedule interviews with prospective architects.

To insert new tasks to the existing task list:

1   In the Task Name field, select the cell before the task you want to insert.
2   Choose Insert, New Task.
3   Enter the task information in the inserted row.

You can also select a row and press the Insert key to insert a new row above it.

Deleting tasks

You also might want to delete a task that is not needed. You can delete a task by selecting it and then choosing Edit, Delete Task. You can also delete a task by selecting it and then pressing the Delete key.

Do it!

B-1: Inserting and deleting tasks

Here's how	Here's why
1 Open Task entry 1	This file contains the complete list of tasks. You'll insert and delete some tasks.
2 Select a cell in row 9	(Any cell will do.) You'll insert a row here.
3 Choose **Insert, New Task**	A new row is added.
4 In the Task Name field, enter **Obtain construction permit**	To insert this task in the task list.
Press (TAB)	
In the Duration field, enter **1**	To change the duration value from estimated to accurate.
5 Select a cell in row 5	You'll insert a row here.
Insert a row	Choose Insert, New Task.

6 In the Task Name field, enter
Architect 1

Press   ⬭TAB⬭

In the Duration field, enter **2 hrs**   This is the time set for interviewing the first architect.

7 Select a cell in row 6   You'll insert two rows.

Press   ⬭INSERT⬭   two times

Add tasks and durations as shown

6		Architect 2	2 hrs
7		Architect 3	2 hrs

8 In row 20, select **Level the ground**   You'll delete this task because it is not needed.

Choose **Edit**, **Delete Task**   To delete the task.

9 Open the Save As dialog box   Choose File, Save As.

Edit the File name box to read **My task entry 1**   To save project file with a new name.

Click **Save**

Rearranging the task list

Explanation

While examining the task list, you might find that some tasks need to be rearranged. You can move tasks from one row to another and rearrange them. When you rearrange tasks, Project 2000 automatically reschedules the task list.

You can move tasks in several ways. You can rearrange tasks by cutting them and then pasting them to another row. You can use the Edit menu commands or the buttons on the Standard toolbar to cut and paste. You can also use the mouse to move tasks.

Moving a task by using the mouse

You can use the mouse to move tasks by pointing to the ID field and dragging the row to a new position. When you select the cell in the ID field, you'll see that the entire row is selected.

Do it!   **B-2:   Moving a task**

Here's how	Here's why
1 Click 31	31 is the ID for the task. You'll move this to row 26.
2 Point as shown	<table><tr><td>30</td><td>Woodwork</td><td>3 days</td></tr><tr><td>31</td><td>Flooring</td><td>7 days</td></tr><tr><td>32</td><td>Furnishing</td><td>2 days</td></tr></table>
3 Drag as shown	<table><tr><td>25</td><td>Build the walls</td><td>7 days</td></tr><tr><td>26</td><td>Miscellaneous</td><td>1 day</td></tr><tr><td>27</td><td>Install plumbing fixtures</td><td>4 days</td></tr><tr><td>28</td><td>Install wiring and cable</td><td>3 days</td></tr><tr><td>29</td><td>Plastering</td><td>4 days</td></tr><tr><td>30</td><td>Woodwork</td><td>3 days</td></tr><tr><td>31</td><td>Flooring</td><td>7 days</td></tr><tr><td>32</td><td>Furnishing</td><td>2 days</td></tr></table> To move the task to row 26.
Observe the task list	<table><tr><td>24</td><td>Lay the roof</td><td>8 days</td></tr><tr><td>25</td><td>Build the walls</td><td>7 days</td></tr><tr><td>26</td><td>Flooring</td><td>7 days</td></tr><tr><td>27</td><td>Miscellaneous</td><td>1 day</td></tr><tr><td>28</td><td>Install plumbing fixtures</td><td>4 days</td></tr></table> The task Flooring has been moved to task 26.
4 Click 🖬	(The Save button is on the Standard toolbar.) To update the project file.

Topic C: Creating the Work Breakdown Structure

Explanation

You organize the task list by creating a hierarchical structure. This structured approach is called the *Work Breakdown Structure* (WBS) and is a built-in tool in Project 2000. The project summary task is the highest level of a task list. Project 2000 uses the task IDs to represent the WBS. You can create an outline manually by indenting and outdenting the task list, and Project 2000 automatically creates the WBS. You can use the outline from the WBS to review the major phases of your project. You also need to identify tasks that occur at regular intervals throughout a project. These tasks serve as checkpoints for the project.

Project summary task

The *project summary task* is the highest level of your task list. You use the project summary task to display the objective of your project. This helps you to work toward your goals and meet the objective for your project. The project summary task contains all the other tasks under it as subtasks. When you choose the option to enter the project summary task, Project 2000 assigns the task ID as 0 because it represents the goal. Project 2000 also formats it in bold and in a larger font size. Project 2000 displays the project title that you entered in the Properties dialog box as the project summary task. In the Gantt chart, a gray bar that extends the entire length of the project represents the project summary task.

To add a project summary task:

1   Choose Tools, Options to open the Options dialog box.
2   Click the View tab.
3   Under the Outline options, check Project summary task to include the summary task in the task list.
4   Click OK and observe that a new row has been added in the Gantt table, and its task ID is 0.

Do it!

C-1:   Adding a project summary task

Here's how	Here's why
1 Choose **File, Properties**	To open the Properties dialog box.
Verify that the Summary tab is active	
Observe the Title box	The title of the project is "Building a new office complex."
Click **OK**	To close the dialog box.
2 Select the first cell of any field	You'll add the project summary task to the task list.
3 Choose **Tools, Options...**	To open the Options dialog box.

4	Verify that the View tab is active	
5	Under Outline options, check **Project summary task**	Outline options for 'My task entry 1.mpp' ☑ Indent name ☑ Show summary tasks ☐ Show outline number ☑ Project summary task ☑ Show outline symbol
		You'll display the project summary task in the task list.
	Click **OK**	To close the dialog box.
6	Observe the Gantt table	When you name the project, that name becomes the project summary task.
	Observe the ID field	Project 2000 assigns 0 as the ID for the project summary task.
	Observe the Gantt chart	A gray bar that spans across the entire project represents the project summary task.
7	Update the project file	Click the Save button on the Standard toolbar.

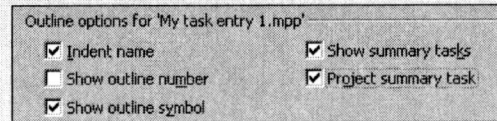

Outlining tasks

Explanation

The WBS represents all the tasks in a hierarchy. The highest level is the objective or goal of the project. The rest of the tasks are broken down to the lowest, manageable levels. The WBS helps you visualize the entire project in terms of scope, cost, resources, and time. To build the WBS, you create a task outline by arranging the tasks into a hierarchy. You establish the hierarchical structure by indenting or outdenting tasks. When you indent a task, you move it one level down. To indent a task, select it and then choose Project, Outline, Indent or click the Indent button on the Formatting toolbar. You can indent or outdent tasks individually or as a group.

When you indent tasks, Project 2000 automatically shifts the indented task to the right. The task that precedes the indented tasks becomes the higher-level task and is called the *summary task*. Indented tasks are called the *subtasks*.

Summary tasks and subtasks

Summary tasks are the next level of tasks under the project summary task and represent the major phases of the project. Each summary task consists of subtasks that represent the activities required to complete the summary task. Project 2000 automatically sums up the subtask details, such as duration and cost, to determine the information required for the summary task. Any changes to the summary task affect the subtasks. For example, if you further indent a summary task, all the subtasks move with it. Similarly, if you delete a summary task, you also delete its subtasks.

When you outdent a task, you move it one level up. You can outdent a task by selecting it and then choosing Project, Outline, Outdent or by clicking the Outdent button on the Formatting toolbar. However, when you outdent a task, Project 2000 makes the subsequent tasks its subtasks. If you do not want subtasks to follow, you can move the outdented task to a new row. You can move the task by using the mouse after you have outdented the task.

Project 2000 provides buttons on the Formatting toolbar to indent and outdent tasks. Exhibit 2-1 shows the buttons used to outline the task list.

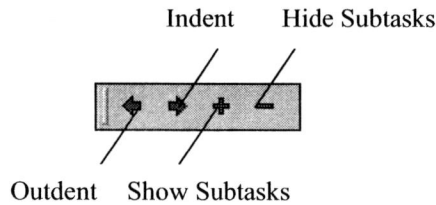

Exhibit 2-1: The Outline buttons on the Formatting toolbar

Do it!

C-2:   Indenting and outdenting tasks

Here's how	Here's why
1 In the Task Name field, select the cell in row 2	You'll indent these tasks to build the WBS.
Drag through row 12 as shown	(table of tasks rows 2-12: Determine the best 3 poter; Determine budget; Interview architects; Architect 1; Architect 2; Architect 3; Select an architect; Prepare first draft plan; Review the plan; Finalize the plan; Obtain construction permit)
2 Click [→]	(The Indent button is on the Formatting toolbar.) To indent the tasks by one level.
3 Observe the task in row 1	1 ⊟ **Design office complex**
	The minus sign that appears indicates that it is a summary task that has subtasks.
Observe the Gantt chart	(Gantt chart Jan 27, '02 – Feb 3, '02)
	The black bar indicates that the task is a summary task.

4	Indent tasks 5 through 7	Select the tasks and click the Indent button.
	Indent tasks 14 through 33	
5	Select **Buy Materials**	(In row 16.) You'll outdent this task.
6	Click ⬅	The Outdent button is on the Formatting toolbar.
7	Outdent tasks 19, 22, 27	Select the task and click the Outdent button.
8	Update the project file	

Hiding subtasks

Explanation

After you have created an outline, tasks are divided into summary tasks and subtasks. Project 2000 allows you to expand or collapse the task list to view different levels of task information. To focus on the main objectives, you can collapse the task list to show only the summary tasks. This makes it easy for you to review the major phases of your project.

When you create an outline, Project 2000 displays an icon to the left of the task name. It can be either a plus sign or a minus sign. A minus sign next to the task name indicates that there are subtasks under it and they are currently shown. You can hide the subtasks by clicking the minus sign or by choosing Project, Outline, Hide Subtasks. You can also click the Hide Subtasks button on the Formatting toolbar. When you collapse the list by clicking the minus sign, you'll see that the icon changes to a plus sign. You can click the plus sign to expand the summary task to show all the subtasks under it.

Do it!

C-3:   Hiding subtasks

Here's how	Here's why
1 Click the minus sign as shown	
	To show only the summary task.
2 Observe the task list	All the subtasks for "Design office complex" are hidden and the minus sign changes to a plus sign.
3 Click the minus sign in row 13	To hide all its subtasks.
4 Click the plus sign in rows 1 and 13	To unhide all the subtasks.
5 Update the project file	

Recurring tasks

Explanation

To monitor the project's progress, you might want to conduct review meetings at regular intervals. Project 2000 refers to tasks that occur at regular intervals during the course of the project as *recurring tasks*.

The Gantt chart represents the recurring task as a summary task consisting of subtasks. These subtasks are entered in the Gantt table with dates in the order of their occurrence. Next to the summary task, in the Indicators field, you see the Recurring task icon. The subtasks also have indicators to specify when each recurring task will occur. Task bars appear in the Gantt chart at regular intervals for each recurring task.

To enter recurring tasks:

1 In the Task Name field, select the cell containing the first task.

2 Choose Insert, Recurring Task to open the Recurring Task Information dialog box.

3 In the Task Name box, enter the name of the recurring task.

4 In the Duration box, enter the duration.

5 Under Recurrence pattern, select the time interval.

6 From the week on list, select an option.

7 Check a weekday to specify the day for the task to occur.

8 Under Range of recurrence, in the Start and End by lists, enter the dates to specify the time period across which the recurring task will occur.

9 Click OK.

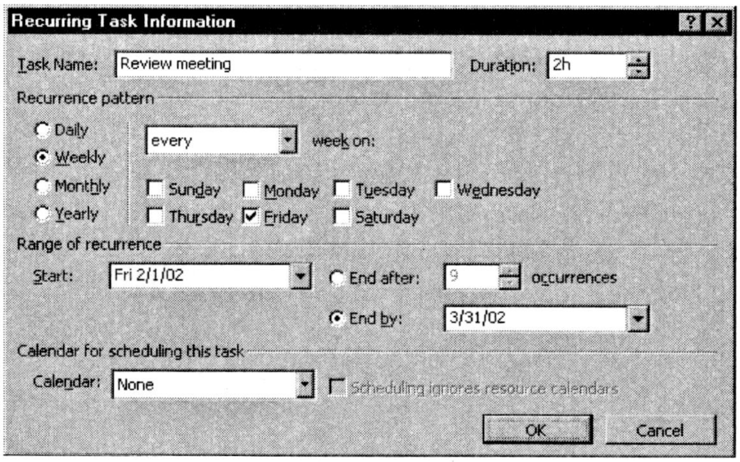

Exhibit 2-2: The Recurring Task Information dialog box

Do it!   **C-4:   Adding recurring tasks**

Here's how	Here's why
1 In the Task Name field, select **Design office complex**	(In row 1.) You'll insert a new row above this row to add recurring task information.
2 Choose **Insert**, **Recurring Task...**	To open the Recurring Task Information dialog box.
3 In the Task Name box, enter **Review meeting**	This will be the name of the recurring task.
In the Duration box, enter **2h**	(Select the Duration box and enter 2h.) To set the duration of the task.
4 Under Recurrence pattern, verify that Weekly is selected	By default, Project 2000 sets recurring tasks to happen weekly.
Under Recurrence pattern, in the week on list, verify that every is selected	
Check **Friday**	To review the layout plan every Friday.
5 Under Range of recurrence, in the Start list, verify that Fri 2/1/02 is selected	By default, Project 2000 assigns the start date of the project as the first occurrence of the recurring task.
Under Range of recurrence, in the End by list, edit the date to be **3/31/02**	To specify the end of the time period for the recurring task.
Click **OK**	To apply the settings as shown in Exhibit 2-2.
6 Observe row 1	

The Recurring task icon appears in the Indicators field.

Point as shown	

A ScreenTip appears.

7 Click the plus sign	(Next to the task Review meeting.) Project 2000 automatically creates a recurring task list, scheduling the task to occur every Friday until 3/31/02.
8 Update the project file	

Topic D: Customizing WBS codes

Explanation

WBS depicts the hierarchy of tasks in your project. Each task has a single, unique WBS code that shows the level of each task and its position in the hierarchy. You can customize WBS codes to view them in a format that suits your needs.

Viewing WBS codes

You use the WBS code to know the level at which a task exists in a hierarchy. For example, the tasks Review meetings and Design office complex are the main tasks under the project summary task. Thus, they have the WBS code 1 and 2 respectively. The tasks Determine the best 3 potential architects and Determine budget are the subtasks of the task Design office complex. Therefore, they have the WBS code 2.1 and 2.2 respectively (as shown in Exhibit 2-3). The Gantt table does not display the WBS codes by default. You can view the WBS codes by inserting a new column into the Gantt table.

To view WBS codes:

1 Choose Insert, Column to open the Column Definition dialog box.
2 From the Field name list, select WBS.
3 Click OK to close the Column Definition dialog box.

WBS code field

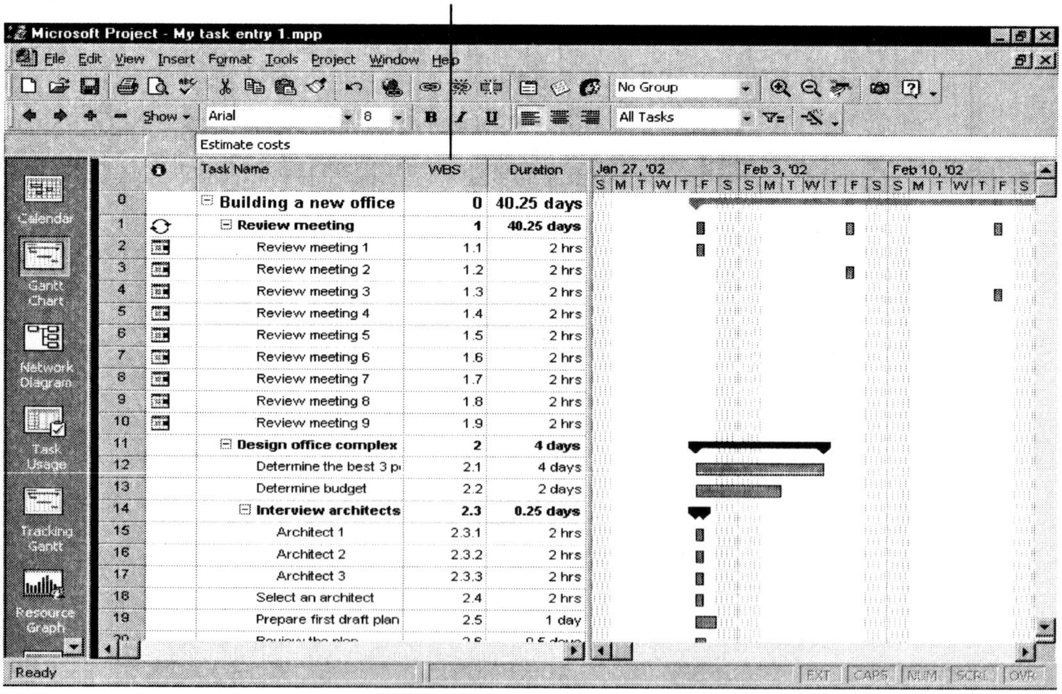

Exhibit 2-3: The WBS codes

Do it!

D-1:   Viewing WBS codes

Here's how	Here's why
1 In the Duration field, select any cell	You'll insert a new field to the left of this field.
2 Choose **Insert, Column...**	To open the Column Definition dialog box.
3 From the Field name list, select **WBS**	You'll view WBS codes.
4 Click **OK**	
Observe the Gantt table	A new field displaying WBS codes appears.
5 Update the project file	

Defining a WBS code

Explanation

The WBS code can include letters as well as numbers. Project 2000, by default, uses the outline numbers as the WBS coding system (as shown in Exhibit 2-3). In this system, the WBS code assigned to a specific task changes as you insert or delete tasks. But, if you define a *mask* for the WBS codes, the WBS code will not change unless you move the task to a different summary task or change the level of the task in the hierarchy. A mask is a pattern of characters used to control the elimination or retention of the WBS code.

To define a WBS code:

1 Choose Project, WBS, Define Code to open the WBS Code Definition dialog box.
2 From the Sequence field, select the format that you want.
3 From the Length field, select the length you want.
4 From the Separator field, select the character that you want.
5 Click OK to close the Code Definition dialog box.

D-2:   Defining and applying WBS codes

Here's how	Here's why
1 Choose **Project, WBS, Define Code...**	To open the WBS Code Definition dialog box.
2 In the Sequence field, verify that the first cell is selected	It displays a drop-down list.
From the list, select **Uppercase Letters (ordered)**	To change the code string of the first level task to a character format.
3 In the Length field, select the first cell.	
From the list, select **1**	To specify the maximum number of characters in the first-level code string.
Observe the Level field	The level is set to 1.
4 In the Separator field, select the first cell	
From the list, select **/**	To specify the character that separates the code string from one level to the next.
5 Observe the Code preview	A preview of the new WBS code for the first-level tasks appears.
6 Enter the WBS code format for levels 2 and 3 as shown	

Level	Sequence	Length	Separator
1	Uppercase Letters (ordered)	1	/
2	Lowercase Letters (ordered)	1	-
3	Numbers (ordered)	1	.

7 Click **OK**	To apply the new WBS code.
Observe the WBS codes in the Gantt table	
8 Update and close the project file	

Unit Summary: Working with tasks

Topic A   In this unit, you learned how to **enter** task information in Gantt Chart view. You learned to **create** a task list by entering task details in the Gantt table.

Topic B   Then, you learned to **modify** the task list by **inserting** new tasks and **deleting** some others. You also learned how to use the mouse to **move** a task in the task list.

Topic C   Next, you learned how to **arrange** tasks in an outline by building the **Work Breakdown Structure (WBS)**. You also learned to add **project summary task** information to the task list by using the Options dialog box. Then, you learned how to **indent**, **outdent**, and **hide subtasks** by using the buttons on the **Formatting** toolbar. Finally, you learned to add a **recurring task** to the task list by using the **Recurring Task Information** dialog box.

Topic D   Finally, you learned to **view WBS codes** by inserting a new column into the Gantt table. You also learned to **define** and **apply WBS codes**.

Independent practice activity

1 Open **Practice entry** (from the Student Data folder).

2 Observe the start date of the project (the project start date should be 10/1/02).

3 Enter the task information (as shown in Exhibit 2-4).

4 Insert a task called **Obtain approval** as the seventh row. Set the duration as 1 day.

5 Delete the task in row 13.

6 Move the task from row 12 to row 4.

7 Add the **project summary task**.

8 Indent tasks 2 through 8, 10 through 21, and then tasks 14 through 16, and 18 through 21.

9 Outdent task 5.

10 Hide the subtasks of the summary task in row 9. (Hint: Click the minus sign next to the summary task.)

11 Add '**Review market demand**' as a recurring task above 'Market analysis.' Set the duration to 2 hrs and set it to occur weekly every Monday. Specify the Range of recurrence from 10/1/02 to 11/30/02. (Hint: Select a cell in row 1, and choose Insert, Recurring Task.)

12 Unhide the subtasks of the summary task in row 1 and 18. (Hint: Click the plus sign next to the summary task.)

13 Insert a column before the Task Name field to view the WBS code.

14 Define a WBS code to set the Sequence of first-level task option to uppercase letters of length 1 and set the separator field to '/'. (Hint: From the Sequence list, select Uppercase Letters (ordered)).

15 Save the project file as **My practice entry** without a baseline.

16 Close the project file.

18		Manage inventory	1 day
19		Send to warehouse	3 days
20		Send to suppliers	3 days
21		Deliver to market	3 days

Exhibit 2-4: The task list after Step 3 of the Independent practice activity

Unit 3
Scheduling tasks

Complete this unit, and you'll know how to:

A Create task relationships by linking and adding lead-time to tasks in Gantt Chart view.

B Explore Network Diagram view and modify the task relationships in it.

C Use the Task Information dialog box to add advanced task information.

Topic A: Setting up task links

Explanation

As a project manager, you have to schedule tasks to complete your project on time. *Scheduling* in a project refers to the timing and sequencing of tasks. As you enter tasks and other related information in the task list, Project 2000 automatically schedules each task on the basis of the project start date. Because tasks in a project are related to each other, it's important to sequence them according to their relationships. To do this, you link the tasks. After you have linked the tasks, you might find that the end date of the project exceeds your planned date. You can address this by adding lead-time to a task or by unlinking some tasks so that the end date meets your plans.

Establishing task links

Project 2000 schedules each task based on the project's start date specified in the Project Information dialog box, and the task's duration. However, in real life, all tasks do not start on the same date because of *dependencies* between tasks. Dependencies between tasks define the way in which two tasks are linked. By default, Project 2000 creates a finish-to-start task dependency such that the start of the second task depends on the finish of the first task.

In the life cycle of a project, the output of one task is the input for another task. As a project manager, you establish links between the tasks to indicate the task dependencies. For example, the output of the task Plan office layout is the input for the task Begin construction. This means that the task Begin construction can begin only after the task Plan office layout is complete.

Predecessor-successor link

When you establish a task link, the task that starts or finishes before another task can begin is called a *predecessor* task. The task that cannot start or finish until the start or completion of a previous task is called a *successor* task.

You can link tasks by selecting the tasks and then choosing Edit, Link Tasks or by clicking the Link Tasks button on the Standard toolbar. When you link tasks, you'll see that a blue line links the task bars in the Gantt chart. After you link tasks, Project 2000 schedules them according to these links.

You might want to view the task bar for the selected task in the Gantt chart. Each task bar graphically represents the corresponding task. By viewing the task bar, you can visualize when the task starts and finishes. Because the Gantt chart doesn't display the entire chart detail, it becomes difficult when you want to see the task bar for a particular task and its links. To avoid this, you select the task name and then click the Go To Selected Task button on the Standard toolbar to view the task bar.

Do it!

A-1: Linking tasks

Here's how	Here's why
1 Open Linking	From the Student Data folder.
2 In the Task Name field, select tasks 11 through 43	You'll link them in sequence so that Project 2000 schedules the tasks.
3 Click [icon]	(The Link Tasks button is on the Standard toolbar.) To establish links between the tasks.
4 Observe the Gantt chart	The tasks are linked as indicated by the link arrows.
Deselect the cells	
5 Observe the Gantt table	Project 2000 automatically schedules the dates according to the duration.
6 Select **Office complex complete**	(In row 43.) You'll check the finish date.
7 Click [icon]	(The Go To Selected Task button is on the Standard toolbar.) To view the task bar for the selected task.
Observe the Finish Date of the last task	This will also be the finish date of the project. Project 2000 automatically calculates the finish date of the last task as the finish date of the project.
8 Save the project file as **My linking**	

Lead versus lag time

Explanation

In your task list, you might have a task that can start before the completion of its predecessor. In such situations, you can reschedule your tasks, and as a result, complete the tasks earlier. You can schedule these tasks to be concurrent by adding *lead time* or *lag time* information. Lag time is the delay that adds extra time after the completion of the task. For example, you can add lag time to the task Build the pillars. This adds extra time for the concrete to set before you begin with the next task Lay the roof.

Lead time is the amount of time from the start of the predecessor task after which a successor task can begin. Therefore, the predecessor task leads the successor task by the amount of time from its start date. For example, when the task Install wire and cables is 80% complete, you can schedule the next or successor task to begin. As a result, you fix 80% lead time to the task Install wire and cables. Alternatively, you can also calculate lead time as negative lag time. When this occurs, you calculate the amount of time left for the task to complete. Therefore, a successor task can begin only when its predecessor is 20% from completion.

You enter lag or lead time information by double-clicking the link line between the tasks. The Task Dependency dialog box appears and you can specify the amount of time in the lag box. To enter lead time, you enter a negative value in the dialog box. To enter lag time, you enter a positive value.

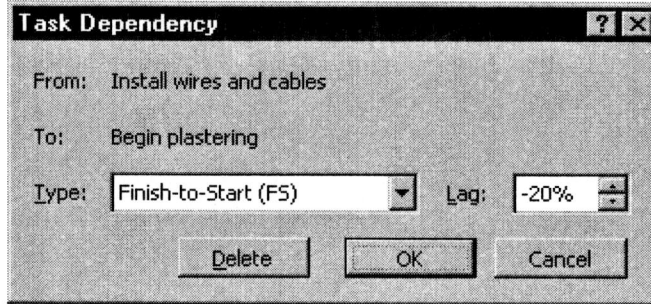

Exhibit 3-1: Adding lead time in the Task Dependency dialog box

<table>
<tr><td>*Do it!*</td><td colspan="2">**A-2:**   **Adding lead time to a task**</td></tr>
</table>

Here's how	Here's why
1 Select **Install wires and cables**	(In row 39.) You'll add lead time to this task.
Click	To view the task bar.
2 Double-click the link line between tasks 39 and 40	To open the Task Dependency dialog box.
3 In the Lag box, enter **−20%**	This will allow the task in row 40 to begin when the task in row 39 is 80% complete.
4 Click **OK**	To close the dialog box.
5 Observe the link line	It indicates that the task Begin plastering starts when the task Install wires and cable is 80% complete.
6 Update the project file	

Unlinking tasks

Explanation   As a project manager, you can select tasks that run independently and in parallel. When you unlink such tasks, by default, Project 2000 schedules them to start the same day. As a result, you can shorten the duration of your project. For example, after linking all tasks, you find that the tasks Rent tools and equipment and Purchase materials can be done independently and run in parallel. So, you unlink them.

You can unlink tasks by selecting the tasks and choosing Edit, Unlink Tasks or by clicking the Unlink Tasks button on the Standard toolbar.

Using the Go To dialog box

When you have a long task list, you can quickly go to a specific task by choosing Edit, Go To. The Go To dialog box appears and you can specify the task ID that you want to view. You can also open the Go To dialog box by pressing F5 key or by pressing the Ctrl + G key combination.

Do it! ## A-3: Unlinking tasks

Here's how	Here's why
1 Choose **Edit, Go To...**	To open the Go To dialog box.
In the ID box, enter 27	
Click **OK**	To go to task 27 directly.
2 In the Task Name field, select tasks 27 and 28	You'll unlink these tasks because these are independent tasks.
3 Observe the Gantt chart	The task link displays a finish-to-start dependency.
4 Click [icon]	(The Unlink Tasks button is on the Standard toolbar.)
Observe the chart	The two bars are aligned under the same start date.
5 Observe the Start field	These tasks will start on the same date.
6 Update the project file	

Topic B: Working in Network Diagram view

Explanation

You can use Network Diagram view to see the complete graphical view of your project. It helps you visualize and analyze the task details and the links between them. The manner in which the Network Diagram view displays the task details makes it easy to modify task links.

Network Diagram view

Project 2000 allows you to switch between Gantt Chart and Network Diagram views without requiring you to re-enter the task information. Working in Gantt Chart view can become difficult if you want to see both the task details and the link between its predecessor and successor. Gantt Chart view does not display the complete information on either pane. Network Diagram view displays project tasks with their dependencies. Boxes called nodes represent tasks. Lines connect the nodes to indicate the task links or dependencies. The summary tasks are represented by a shadow box and solid-bordered boxes represent all the subtasks. Each node displays the five fields of a task: the name, ID, duration, start, and finish dates. Each node is connected to a predecessor and successor.

Zooming the Network Diagram view

By default, Network Diagram view displays each node in 100% zoom. However, you cannot see the complete flowchart, and you'll have to scroll horizontally and vertically. You zoom the view to fit in more nodes, and to get an overview of the tasks and their links. You can view more tasks by using the Zoom dialog box and selecting a zoom size. You can also zoom the view by clicking the Zoom Out button on the Standard toolbar.

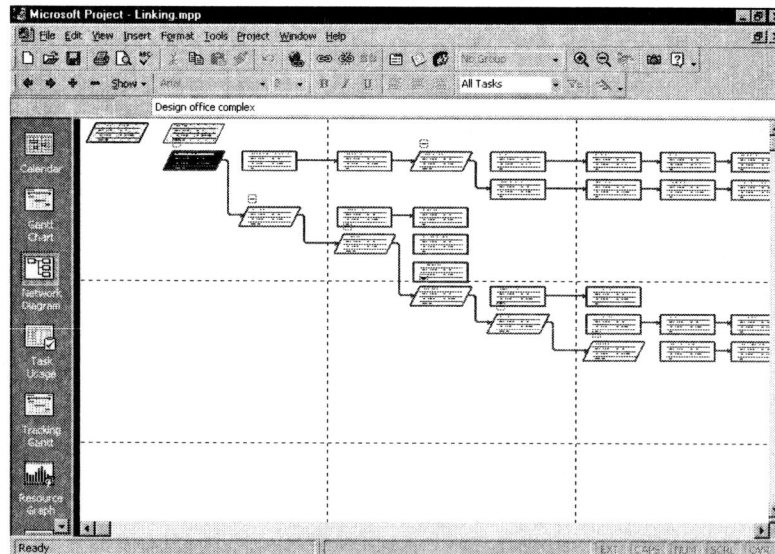

Exhibit 3-2: The Network Diagram view of the project, reduced to 25%

Do it!

B-1:   Exploring Network Diagram view

Here's how	Here's why
1 In the Task Name field, select **Design office complex**	(In row 11.) You'll view the Network Diagram from this task.
2 Click ▣	(The Network Diagram button is on the View bar.) To switch to Network Diagram view.
3 Observe the Network Diagram view	Project 2000 displays the project information in the form of a flow chart in Network Diagram view.
4 Scroll horizontally	All the tasks are represented in a box and an arrow represents the link between them.
5 Observe the summary task	**Design office complex** Start: 2/1/02 ID: 11 Finish: 2/14/02 Dur: 9.5 days Comp: 0%

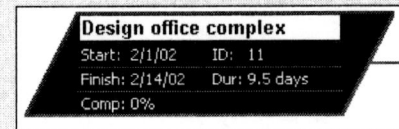

A shaded box represents the summary task. |
| 6   Observe the subtask | **Determine the best 3 potenti** Start: 2/1/02 ID: 12 Finish: 2/6/02 Dur: 4 days Res:

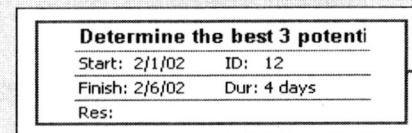

A red-bordered box represents the subtask. |
| 7   Choose **View, Zoom...** | To open the Zoom dialog box. |
| Select **Custom** | |
| In the Custom box, enter **25** | Zoom

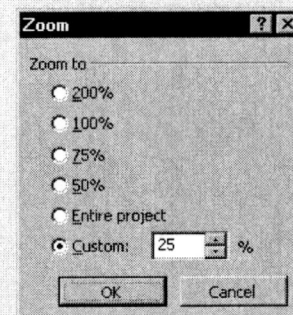

Zoom to
○ 200%
○ 100%
○ 75%
○ 50%
○ Entire project
● Custom: 25 %
OK   Cancel |
| Click **OK** | To zoom the view of the chart to 25% (as shown in Exhibit 3-2). |

8	Observe the dashed lines	They indicate page breaks that help you see how the printout will paginate.
9	Click 🔍 twice	(The Zoom In button is on the Standard toolbar.) To enlarge the view.
10	Update the project file	

Modifying task links

Explanation   With Network Diagram view, you can easily view the links and dependencies between tasks. You can also view the occurrence of a task within the project to analyze the task links. After analyzing the task relationships, you might find that some tasks do not actually depend on each other as indicated in the schedule. As a result, you can reschedule your project by modifying the task links. When you modify a task relationship, Project 2000 automatically recalculates the schedule of the project.

Task relationships

There are different task relationships provided by Project 2000. When you link tasks, you can specify the dependency between them. By default, Project 2000 specifies a Finish-to-Start link. The following table provides the task dependencies with their descriptions.

Dependency	Example	Implies
Finish-to-Start (FS)		Task B cannot start unless Task A is finished.
Start-to-Start (SS)		Task B cannot start unless Task A starts.
Finish-to-Finish (FF)		Task B cannot finish unless Task A is finished.
Start-to-Finish (SF)		Task B cannot finish unless Task A starts.

You modify a task dependency by double-clicking the link line. For example, the link between the summary tasks Design office complex and Plan office layout can be modified to have a Start-to-Start dependency because these tasks can be done concurrently. When you modify the task dependency between them, all the subtasks are rescheduled to run parallel. This saves a lot of time because all the subtasks run parallel and you finish the project earlier. To modify a task dependency, you double-click the link line and the Task Dependency dialog box appears. From the Type list, select the type of task relationship that you want to specify.

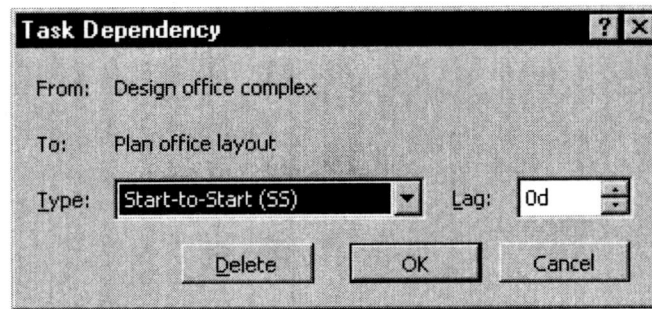

Exhibit 3-3: The Task Dependency dialog box

Do it!

B-2: Modifying a task link in Network Diagram view

Here's how	Here's why
1 Double-click the link line between Design office complex and Plan office layout	You'll modify the link between them. The Task Dependency dialog box appears.
2 Observe the Type box	By default, Project 2000 links tasks with a Finish-to-Start relationship.
3 In the Type list, click the drop-down arrow	 The list provides four types of relationship.
Select **Start-to-Start**	(As shown in Exhibit 3-3.) To schedule the Design and Plan tasks to run parallel.
Click **OK**	To apply the task dependency type.
4 Click [icon]	(The Zoom Out button is on the Standard toolbar.)
5 Observe the network diagram	The Design summary task and all its subtasks are bordered in blue to indicate the new task dependency.
6 Update the project file	

Topic C: Working with advanced task options

Explanation

As a project manager, you've learned to plan a project by creating a task list, linking tasks, and defining task dependencies to manage and control your project. To make it progress efficiently and effectively, you also have to consider factors such as task duration, work effort on each task, and constraints. To use Project 2000 to schedule the project tasks on the basis of these factors, you have to specify the task information, such as task type and task constraints.

Types of tasks

Tasks can be divided into three types: fixed duration, fixed work, or fixed unit.

A *fixed duration* task has a constant time value. Even if you increase the resources allocated to the task, the duration will remain the same. For example, a task has a fixed duration of 2 days and 2 resources are assigned to it. Even if another resource is added to the task, Project 2000 will not change the duration.

In a *fixed work* task, the total work to be performed has a constant value. The total amount of work performed on a task is the sum of resources used on that task. For example, if 3 resources work an 8-hour schedule for 2 days, the total work performed on the task is 48 hours (3 resources multiplied by 8 hours multiplied by 2 days). Therefore, 48 hours of work is fixed for the task.

A *fixed unit* task has a constant quantity or units of resource value. For example, the tasks that require wood or paint are a fixed unit type because they remain constant.

Do it!

C-1: Inserting a task type

Here's how	Here's why
1 Switch to Gantt Chart view	Click the Gantt Chart button on the View bar.
2 Select **Prepare layout plan**	(In row 24.) You'll mark this task as a fixed duration task.
3 Choose **Project, Task Information...**	To open the Task Information dialog box.
4 Click the **Advanced** tab	

5	From the Task type list, select **Fixed Duration**	To assign the fixed duration type to this task.
	Click **OK**	To apply the settings.
6	Update the project file	

Milestone tasks

Explanation

You might want to identify certain tasks that represent the completion of a major phase or activity in your project as *milestones*. A milestone is a checkpoint in the life cycle of the project. For example, obtaining a construction permit is a milestone because it signifies the end of the initial phase. The next phase, preparing the site for construction, starts only after this task is complete.

You set a milestone by entering it as a task of zero duration. Project 2000 automatically marks any task with zero duration as a milestone.

Do it!

C-2: Setting a milestone

Here's how	Here's why
1 Select **Obtain construction permit**	(In row 22.) You'll set this task as a milestone.
2 Click	(The Task Information button is on the Standard toolbar.) To open the Task Information dialog box.
Verify that the Advanced tab is active	
3 In the Duration box, enter **0d**	To specify the duration as zero days.
Check **Mark task as milestone**	To assign this task as a milestone.
4 Click **OK**	To apply the settings and close the dialog box.

5   Click [icon]   To view the selected task in the Gantt chart.

Observe the Gantt chart

Milestones are indicated as diamond icons in the Gantt chart.

6   Update the project file

Task constraints

Explanation

Constraints are limitations imposed upon tasks in a project. While planning your project, you have to be aware of external factors like deadlines and availability of resources. You can specify task constraints by imposing restrictions. Constraints also allow you to control the start and finish dates of a task. Task constraints affect the project schedule, duration, and flexibility. While rescheduling, Project 2000 prompts the Planning Wizard if it comes across any conflict on task links or the start and finish dates of tasks.

Types of constraints

Project 2000 provides several different task constraints, which are described in the following table.

Constraint	Description
As Late As Possible	It schedules a task to start as late as possible. Project 2000 schedules the task with this constraint from the finish date of the project.
As Soon As Possible	It schedules a task to start as soon as possible. This is the default task constraint used by Project 2000 and schedules a task with this constraint from the start date of the project.
Finish No Earlier Than	It schedules a task to finish on or after a specified date. A task with this constraint cannot finish before the specified date.
Finish No Later Than	It schedules a task to finish on or before a specified date. A task with this constraint cannot finish after the specified date.

Constraint	Description
Must Finish On	It schedules a task to finish on the specified date.
Must Start On	It schedules a task to start on a specified date.
Start No Earlier Than	It schedules a task to start on or after a specified date.
Start No Later Than	It schedules a task to start on or before a specified date.

Do it!

C-3: Setting up a task constraint

Here's how	Here's why
1 Select **Build the foundation**	(In row 31.) You'll set a task constraint.
2 Open the Task Information dialog box	Choose Project, Task Information.
Verify that the Advanced tab is active	
3 Observe the Constraint type box	By default, Project 2000 sets the constraint As Soon As Possible to a task.
4 From the Constraint type list, select **Finish No Later Than**	To set this constraint because the construction can start only after the end of this task.
5 In the Constraint date box, enter **03/05/02**	To specify the end date of the task.
6 Click **OK**	To close the dialog box. The Planning Wizard dialog box appears.
7 Observe the dialog box	It gives you options to work with the scheduling conflict that Project 2000 comes across while setting the constraint.
Select the option as shown	You can: ○ Cancel. No constraint will be set on 'Build the foundation'. ○ Continue, but avoid the conflict by using a Finish No Earlier Than constraint instead. ● Continue. A Finish No Later Than constraint will be set.
Click **OK**	To set the constraint. The Planning Wizard dialog box appears.

8 Select the option as shown	You can: ○ Cancel. Avoid the scheduling conflict. ◉ Continue. Allow the scheduling conflict.
Click **OK**	To allow the scheduling conflict.
9 Observe row 31	A Task constraint icon appears in the first field.
Point as shown	<table><tr><td>30</td><td colspan="2">Excavate for foundation</td><td>10 days</td></tr><tr><td>31</td><td colspan="2">Build the foundation</td><td>12 days</td></tr><tr><td>32</td><td>This task has a 'Finish No Later Than' constraint on Tue 3/5/02.</td><td></td><td>**32 days**</td></tr><tr><td>33</td><td></td><td></td><td>10 days</td></tr></table>
	A ScreenTip appears.
Deselect the cell	
10 Update and close the project file	

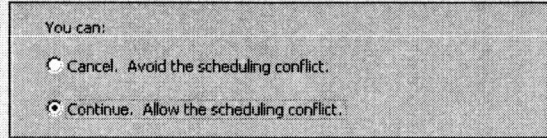

Unit Summary: Scheduling tasks

Topic A   In this unit, you learned to **link** tasks by using the **Link Tasks button** on the Standard toolbar. You learned to add **lead time** to tasks by using the **Task Dependency** dialog box. You also learned to **unlink** tasks by using the **Unlink Tasks button** on the Standard toolbar.

Topic B   Then, you learned to **explore** Network Diagram view by navigating the chart. You also learned to work in Network Diagram view by **modifying** task links.

Topic C   Finally, you learned to work with **advanced task options** by specifying a **task type**. You learned about **milestone tasks** and applied a milestone to the task list. You also learned to work with **task constraints**. You used the **Task Information** dialog box to set all the advanced task options.

Independent practice activity

1   Open **Practice link**.

2   Link tasks 10 through 30.

3   Add a 30% lead time to task 11. (Hint: Click the link line between tasks 11 and 12 and set lead time as a negative percentage.)

4   Unlink tasks 23 through 25.

5   Switch to Network Diagram view.

6   Create a Start-to-Start relationship between tasks Advertise and Distribution.

7   Assign a fixed duration to the task Determine budget. (Hint: Switch to Gantt Chart view.)

8   Assign a Must Finish On constraint to the task Sales training. Specify the finish date as 10/12/02. Allow any scheduling conflicts.

9   Set Obtain approval as a milestone task. (Hint: Set the task duration as zero.)

10   Save the project file as **My practice link**. (Hint: Save without a baseline.)

11   Close the project file.

Unit 4

Managing resources

Complete this unit, and you'll know how to:

A Use the Change Working Time dialog box to create a base calendar for the project.

B Use the Resource Sheet to create a resource pool and assign resources to tasks.

C Enter resource costs in Resource Sheet view and use the Cost table in Gantt Chart view.

Topic A: Creating a base calendar

Explanation

When you add any task-related information, Project 2000 schedules them automatically on the basis of a *base calendar.* A base calendar defines the working days and working hours for a project. After creating a base calendar, you add it to the project to make it the project's calendar.

Base calendar

Every project is linked to a base calendar. Project 2000 provides three calendars: Standard, 24 Hour, and Night Shift. Project 2000 uses the *Standard calendar* as the default base calendar for a project. This calendar uses a Monday through Friday week, working hours from 8 AM to 5 PM, with an hour off at noon, and no holidays. You can use any calendar provided by Project 2000 as your project calendar, or you can create a new base calendar.

Creating a base calendar

Every organization has its own working hours. If your organization's working and nonworking hours differ from the default hours of the base calendar, you can create a new base calendar and link it to the project. You'll also need to specify the holidays your company observes because the default base calendar does not include holidays. This helps you to accurately plan your project.

Project 2000 schedules all the tasks based on the project's new base calendar. When you edit a day as a working day, it reflects across all months. When you edit a day as a nonworking day, it reflects only in that month. Project 2000 also adds holidays and nonworking time during the life cycle of the project.

To create a new base calendar and link it to the project:

1 Choose Tools, Change Working Time to open the Change Working Time dialog box.

2 Click New to open the Create New Base Calendar dialog box.

3 In the Name box, enter a name for your calendar.

4 Select Create New Base Calendar to start with a new calendar. You can also select Make a copy of when you want to edit one of the existing calendars provided by Project 2000.

5 Click OK.

6 Make the necessary changes in the calendar.

7 Specify the working time for the working days that you have added to the calendar.

8 Click OK.

9 Choose Project, Project Information to open the Project Information dialog box to link the new base calendar to the project.

10 From the Calendar list, select the new base calendar that you created. This will now be your project calendar.

When you save your project file, changes to the base calendar are also saved in the project file.

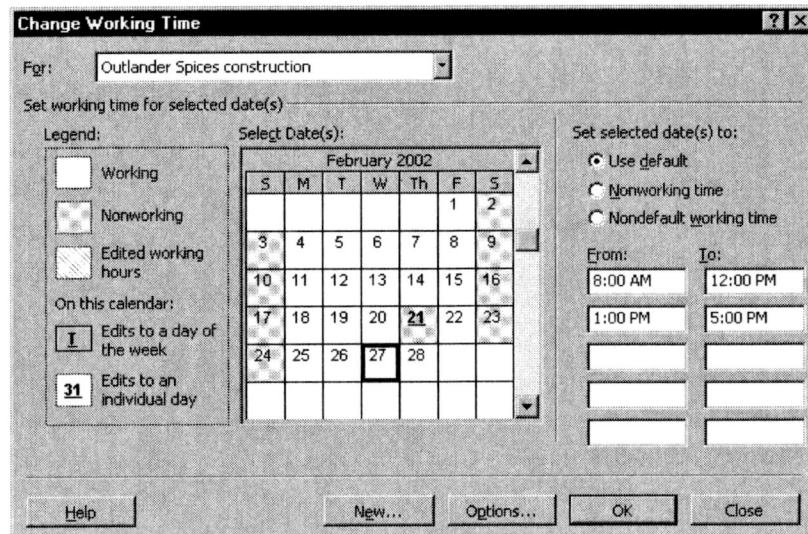

Exhibit 4-1: The Change Working Time dialog box

Do it!

A-1: Creating a new base calendar

Here's how	Here's why
1 Open Resources	You'll create a new base calendar for the project.
2 Choose **Tools, Change Working Time...**	To open the Change Working Time dialog box.
3 Observe the dialog box	It displays the current month and the Standard project calendar with default working hours.
4 Click **New**	To open the Create New Base Calendar dialog box.
Edit the Name box to read **Outlander Spices construction**	This will be the name of the project calendar.
5 Select **Create new base calendar**	To create a new base calendar.
Click **OK**	

6	Observe the For box	The name of the base calendar that you just specified appears.
	In the February 2002 calendar, select **21**	(If necessary, scroll vertically.) To declare it as a nonworking day because it is President's Day.
7	Under Set selected date(s) to, select **Nonworking time**	To set this as a nonworking day.
	Deselect the date	Click any other date.
	Observe the date	Project 2000 automatically changes the date in the Nonworking legend style (as shown in Exhibit 4-1).
8	Scroll to the March 2002 calendar	You'll specify nonworking days for this month.
	In the March 2002 calendar, select **18**	This will be a nonworking day to observe St. Patrick's Day.
	Select **Nonworking time**	To set it as a nonworking day.
9	Mark April 22, 2002 as nonworking day	(In the April 2002 calendar, select 22, and select Nonworking time.) To observe the Outlander Spices founding.
	Click **OK**	To close the dialog box.
	Observe the Microsoft Project dialog box	You will see a list of suggestions to avoid the scheduling conflict on the project.
	Click **OK**	To close the Microsoft Project dialog box.
10	In row 31, observe the task	The task Build the foundation starts on February 18 and finishes on March 5.
11	Choose **Project**, **Project Information...**	To open the Project Information dialog box.
	From the Calendar list, select **Outlander Spices construction**	This will be the new base calendar for the project.
	Click **OK**	To close the dialog box.
12	Observe the task Build the foundation	Project 2000 automatically shifts the start date to February 15 to include one nonworking day in the task's duration because no task is scheduled for February 21.
13	Save the project file as **My resources**	

Topic B: Working with resources and calendars

Explanation

One of the main areas that you, as a project manager, need to focus on during the planning phase of a project is resource availability. You have to determine the resources (people, tools and equipment, and materials) and the quantity of each resource that will be needed for the project. Based on their availability, you assign resources to individual tasks to meet the goals and objectives of the project.

The resource pool

The list of resources required for completing the project efficiently is referred to as the *resource pool*. It is essential to refer to the Work Breakdown Structure, project objectives, and organization policies when you plan your resources. This helps you assign resources based on the skill of the resources, project requirements, and the project cost. Project 2000 allows you to add two kinds of resources to your project plan: *work resources* and *material resources*. A work resource performs work on a task. Some typical examples of work resources are people and equipment. A material resource is an item that is used to perform work on a task. Paint, wood, steel, and fuel are examples of material resources.

Using Resource Sheet view to create a resource pool

You create a resource pool by using *Resource Sheet view*. This view displays the resource information and resembles a spreadsheet with columns and rows. It provides columns in which you can enter resource information such as name, type, material label, initials, group, maximum units, standard and overtime rates, cost, and the calendar it uses. You can review and edit information about any resource in Resource Sheet view.

You enter the resource name in the Name field and the type of resource, such as work or material, in the Type field. You'll enter the unit of measurement for a material resource in the Material label field. For example, if the material is paint, you can enter gallons in the Material label field. You cannot enter a value in this field for a work type resource. You specify the group, such as department, block, or category, to which the resource belongs, in the Group field. By default, the MaxUnits field displays 100%, which indicates the availability of a single resource and its working time. For example, if you have two excavators for your project, then you specify 200% in the MaxUnits field. However, you cannot enter a value in this field for a material resource.

In the Base Calendar field, you assign a calendar to a work resource. By default, Project 2000 assigns the Standard calendar to all work resources. However, you need to apply the new base calendar that you've created if the Standard calendar doesn't apply. You cannot apply a base calendar to a material resource. You'll notice that most of the buttons on the toolbars are not available when you enter information in any of the cells in the Resource sheet. As a result, you need to deselect the cell that contains information before you save the Resource sheet.

Do it!

B-1: Creating a resource pool in Resource Sheet view

Here's how	Here's why
1 Scroll to the bottom of the View bar	(Use the Down arrow button on the View bar.) You'll use the resource sheet to create a resource pool.
2 Click	(The Resource Sheet button is on the View bar.) To switch to Resource Sheet view.
3 Observe the view	This view looks like a spreadsheet with resource fields as column headings.
4 In the first Resource Name field, enter **Kathy Sinclair**	This will be the first resource name for the project.
Press TAB	To move to the next field.
Observe the Type field	Project 2000, by default, sets the resource type to Work.
5 Press TAB twice	You cannot enter a Material label for Work-type resources.
Observe the Initials field	Project 2000 automatically provides initials for the resource name.
6 In the Group field, enter **Project management consultant**	This resource is hired by Outlander Spices to oversee the entire project.
Observe the other fields	Project 2000 provides all default values to the fields.
7 In the Resource Name field, select the second cell	You'll add the details for the second resource in this cell.
Enter **Jack Thomas**	This will be the second resource name.
In the Group field, enter **Sales**	This resource will be in the Sales group.
8 In the Resource Name field, select the third cell	You'll add details for the third resource in this cell.
Enter **Paint**	This will be the third resource name.
Press TAB	To move to the Type field.

9	Click the drop-down arrow and select **Material**	To set this resource as a material resource.
	In the Material Label field, enter **gallon**	This will be the unit of measurement for this resource.
	In the Group field, enter **Purchased**	This resource will be in the Purchased group.
10	In the Base Calendar field, select the first cell	The cell changes to a list box.
	Click the drop-down arrow and select the option shown	

Accrue At	Base Calendar	
Prorated	Standard	▼
Pror	24 Hours	
	Night Shift	
Pror	Outlander Spices constru	
	Standard	

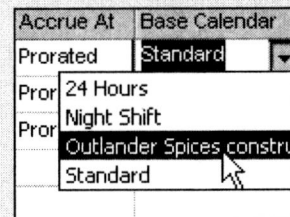

The company uses 'Outlander Spices construction' as its base calendar.

	Press (↵ ENTER)	
11	From the drop-down list, select **Outlander Spices construction**	To assign this calendar as the base calendar for Jack Thomas.
12	Press (↵ ENTER)	
	Observe the Base Calendar field	You cannot assign a base calendar to a material resource.
	Deselect the cell	Click anywhere on the sheet.
13	Update and close the project file	Save without a baseline.

Resource calendar

Explanation

When creating a resource list in Resource Sheet view, you also assign the project's base calendar for each resource. Each resource is assigned the project's base calendar so that Project 2000 can schedule the nonworking time for the resources. However, if the working and nonworking time of the project does not coincide with the availability of a resource, you can create a *resource calendar* for it. A resource calendar contains information that is specific to a resource. For example, Jack Thomas's resource calendar needs to reflect his vacation. You can create a resource calendar for Jack that reflects the nonworking days of his vacation.

To create a resource calendar:

1 In Resource Sheet view, under the Name field, select the resource to which you want to assign a calendar.

2 Click the Resource Information button.

3 Click the Working Time tab.

4 Make the necessary changes in the calendar.

5 Click OK.

Do it!

B-2: Creating a resource calendar

Here's how	Here's why
1 Open Resources 1	This resource sheet contains complete information about the resources for the project. You'll create a resource calendar for one of the resources.
2 In the Resource Name field, select **Jack Thomas**	You'll change the calendar for this resource.
3 Click [icon]	(The Resource Information button is on the Standard toolbar.) To open the Resource Information dialog box.
4 Click the **Working Time** tab	
5 In the Base calendar list, verify that Outlander Spices construction is selected	This is the base calendar for all resources.
6 Scroll to the April 2002 calendar	You'll set a nonworking day specifically for Jack.
7 Select the date shown	

	April 2002					
S	M	T	W	Th	F	S
		1	2	3	4	5	6
7	8	9	10	11	12	13
14	15	16	17	18	19	20
21	22	23	24	25	26	27
28	29	30				

Here's how	Here's why
Select **Nonworking time**	To mark April 19 as a nonworking day for Jack.
8 Click **OK**	To apply the new resource calendar. (Allow the scheduling conflict, if the Planning Wizard appears.)
9 Save the project file as **My resources 1**	Save without a baseline, if the Planning Wizard appears.

Assigning resources

Explanation

After you have planned the tasks and created the resource pool, you assign resources to the tasks because resources are used to complete the tasks of your project. You assign resources to the tasks in Gantt Chart view.

To assign resources:

1 Switch to Gantt Chart view.
2 Select the task to which you want to assign a resource.
3 Choose Tools, Resources, Assign Resources to open the Assign Resources dialog box.
4 Select one or more resources by clicking on the resource names.
5 Click Assign to assign the resources to the task.
6 Click Close to close the dialog box.

You can also assign resources by clicking the Assign Resources button on the Standard toolbar.

Do it!

B-3:   Assigning resources to tasks

Here's how	Here's why
1 Switch to Gantt Chart view	Click the Gantt Chart button on the View bar.
2 Press (F5)	To open the Go To dialog box.
In the ID box, enter **12**	To go to row 12.
Click **OK**	To close the dialog box.
3 Click	(The Assign Resources button is on the Standard toolbar.) To open the Assign Resources dialog box. You'll add resources to the task.
In the Resources from list, verify that Kathy Sinclair is selected	This is the resource that you'll assign to the task.
4 Click **Assign**	To assign the resource. Notice the Units field. It indicates that the resource is utilized 100% for the task.
Click **Close**	To close the dialog box.
5 Observe the Gantt Chart	The resource name appears to the right of the task bar.

6	Scroll horizontally to the last field of the Gantt table	
	Observe the Resource Names field	In the Resource Names field, 'Kathy Sinclair' appears.
7	Select **Excavate for foundation**	In row 30.
8	Click [icon]	To open the Assign Resources dialog box.
9	From the Name list, select **Joe Simmons**	You'll assign this resource to the task.
	Click **Assign**	To assign the resource.
	Click **Close**	To close the dialog box.
	Observe the Resource Names field	In the Resource Names field, 'Joe Simmons' appears.
10	Update the project file	Save without a baseline if the Planning Wizard appears.

Creating a task calendar

Explanation

You might want to specify working time that differs from the project calendar or the calendars of assigned resources. For example, resources may be available 8 hours a day from Monday to Friday. However, the tools for the tasks might require maintenance every Friday. You can use the task calendar to define a unique or specific exception for scheduling individual tasks that requires equipment that runs during nonworking time or requires maintenance during working time.

By default, Project 2000 does not assign any calendar to a task. It schedules the task according to the working and nonworking times in the project calendar. However, when a task calendar or a resource calendar is assigned to a task, it takes precedence over the project calendar. You might have a task calendar and a calendar for the resource assigned to the task. When this occurs, Project 2000 allows you to decide which calendar will have precedence over the other.

Do it!   **B-4:   Creating and applying a task calendar**

Here's how	Here's why
1 Choose **Tools, Change Working Time...**	To open the Change Working Time dialog box.
2 Click **New**	To open the Create New Base Calendar dialog box.
Edit the Name box to read **Construction equipment**	This will be the name of the project calendar.
3 Verify that Make a copy of is selected	
4 In the calendar list, verify that Outlander Spices construction is selected	To create a copy of the Outlander Spices construction calendar.
5 Click **OK**	To close the Create New Base Calendar dialog box.
Observe the For box	The name of the base calendar that you just specified appears.
6 Mark **February 15, 2002** as a nonworking day	(In the February 2002 calendar, select 15, and select Nonworking time.) To set this day for equipment maintenance.
7 Click **OK**	To close the Change Working Time dialog box.
8 Verify that Excavate for foundation is selected	(In row 30.) You'll apply a calendar to this task.
Observe the task	The task Excavate for foundation starts on February 11 and finishes on February 25.
9 Choose **Project, Task Information...**	To open the Task Information dialog box.
10 Verify that the **Advanced** tab is active	
11 From the Calendar list, select **Construction equipment**	You'll apply this calendar to the task.

12 Check **Scheduling ignores resource calendars**	To specify that the task calendar takes precedence over the resource calendar.
13 Click **OK**	
Observe the indicator field in row 30	
	The Task calendar icon appears.
Point as shown	
	A ScreenTip appears.
Observe the Finish date field	Project 2000 automatically shifts the finish date to February 26 to include one nonworking day in the task duration because the equipment is not available on February 15 to complete the task.
14 Update the project file	Save without a baseline if the Planning Wizard appears.

Topic C: Working with resource costs

Explanation

During the planning phase of your project, you also estimate resource costs. You need to estimate the cost very carefully to determine the budget for the project. Project 2000 helps you calculate resource costs at both the individual and overall level of the project. You enter the resource cost in either the resource sheet or the Cost table.

Resource and task costs

While planning your project, you assign costs to each resource and task to determine the project budget. You also determine the cost to your organization to estimate the profit. When you assign costs, Project 2000 calculates the overall cost of the project, and the cost of individual tasks and resources. However, you might have different costs for different types of resources in your project.

Types of costs

Resource and task costs can be broadly divided as *fixed* or *variable* costs. A fixed cost remains the same despite resources being added or taken away; for example, legal fees, architect's fees, and permit fees.

A variable cost varies with the frequency and amount of time a resource is used. For example, the construction service company hires an excavator on an hourly basis. This cost varies by the number of hours the company needs the excavator.

Project 2000 provides three types of variable cost - *standard cost, overtime cost*, and *per use cost*. Standard cost is the cost incurred to pay a resource for the hours worked on a task during the standard working hours as defined in a project. Overtime cost is the cost incurred to pay a resource for the hours worked during the overtime working hours as defined in a project. Per use cost is the cost incurred for the use of every unit of a resource in a task. Per use cost is commonly used for resource materials like gravel, wood, and paint. Project 2000 multiplies the per use cost of the materials by the number of units of the material used for the task to calculate the total cost for the task and the resource.

Do it!

C-1: Entering resource cost

Here's how	Here's why
1 Switch to Resource Sheet view	(Click the Resource Sheet button on the View bar.) You'll assign costs to resources.
2 In the Std. Rate field, select the first cell	To enter a standard rate for the resource Kathy Sinclair.
Enter **62.5**	This is the standard rate to be paid to Kathy, which is $62.50/hr.
3 In the Std. Rate field, select the second cell	To enter the standard rate for Jack Thomas.
Enter **50**	$50.00/hr is the standard rate to be paid to Jack.

4 Enter other standard rates as shown

Curt Allen	Work		C	External	100%	$35.00/hr
Eric	Work		E	Finance	100%	$17.00/hr
Ann Salinski	Work		A	Finance	100%	$43.75/hr
Susan Gianni	Work		S	Business cc	100%	$100.00/hr
Joe Simmons	Work		J	External	100%	$30.00/hr

5 Enter **12** as Cost/Use for Paint — (In row 13.)

Enter **10** as Cost/Use for Wood — (In row 14.)

Deselect the cell

6 Update the project file — Save without a baseline if the Planning Wizard appears.

The Cost table

Explanation

Project 2000 provides predefined project tables that can be applied to both tasks and resource views. The *Cost table* in Gantt Chart view is one of them. The Cost table displays the cost-related information of the project tasks, which includes fixed cost, baseline cost, variance, actual cost, and remaining cost. You need to switch to the Cost table in Gantt Chart view to see the fixed cost of resources. Exhibit 4-2 displays the Cost table with Fixed Cost and Total Cost for tasks.

You switch to the Cost table in Gantt Chart view by choosing View, Table, Cost. The Total Cost field displays the cost for the task based on the standard rate of the resource. Project 2000 multiplies the value in the Std. Rate field for a resource and the number of days the resource is working on the task. For example, the standard cost of Kathy is $62.50/hr. She is assigned the task Determine the best 3 potential architects for 4 days. The total cost for this task is $2000 ($62.50 multiplied by 8 multiplied by 4).

	Task Name	Fixed Cost	Fixed Cost Accrual	Total Cost
1	⊞ **Reviewing layout plan**	**$0.00**	**Prorated**	**$0.00**
11	⊟ **Designing**	**$0.00**	**Prorated**	**$62,000.00**
12	Determining budget	$0.00	Prorated	$0.00
13	Determining the best 3 ı	$0.00	Prorated	$2,000.00
14	⊟ **Interviewing archite**	**$0.00**	**Prorated**	**$60,000.00**
15	Architect 1	$0.00	Prorated	$0.00
16	Architect 2	$0.00	Prorated	$0.00
17	Architect 3	$0.00	Prorated	$0.00
18	Selecting an archite	$60,000.00	Prorated	$60,000.00
19	Preparing first draft pla	$0.00	Prorated	$0.00

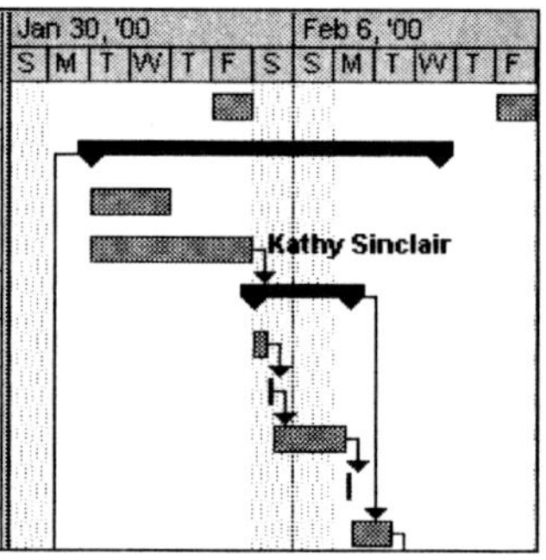

Exhibit 4-2: The Cost table displaying cost for tasks

Do it!

C-2: Using the Cost table

Here's how	Here's why
1 Switch to Gantt Chart view	You'll use the Cost table in this view.
2 Choose **View**, **Table: Entry**, **Cost**	To switch to Cost table view.
3 In row 12, observe the Total Cost field	The total cost for the task Determine the best 3 potential architects is $2000 because Kathy who is assigned for this task has a standard cost of $62.50/hr.
4 In row 18, select the Fixed Cost field	You'll enter a fixed cost for the task, select an architect, because the architect gets a fixed amount for the project.
Enter **60,000**	$60,000.00 is the fixed cost for this task. The total cost is the same.
Press (↵ ENTER)	
Observe the Total Cost field for the task Design office complex	(In row 11.) Project 2000 sums up the total cost for all subtasks and displays it as the total cost for the summary task.
5 Choose **View**, **Table: Cost**, **Entry**	To switch to Entry table view.
6 Update and close the project file	Save without a baseline if the Planning Wizard appears.

Unit Summary: Managing resources

Topic A   In this unit, you learned to create a **new base calendar** by using the **Change Working Time** command.

Topic B   Then, you learned to create a **resource pool** by using **Resource Sheet** view. You created a **resource calendar** for a resource and also learned to **assign resources** to tasks by using the **Assign Resources** button on the Standard toolbar. You also learned to create a **task calendar**.

Topic C   Finally, you learned to work with **resource costs** by entering them in Resource Sheet view and learned to **assign fixed cost** by using the **Cost table** in Gantt Chart view.

Independent practice activity

1   Open **Practice resources**.

2   Open the Change Working Time dialog box.

3   Create a new base calendar, **Product calendar**.

4   Set November 22, 2002 as a nonworking day.

5   Assign Product Calendar as the new project calendar. (Hint: Choose Project, Project Information.)

6   Switch to Resource Sheet view.

7   Enter the resource information as shown in Exhibit 4-3. Assign the Product calendar to each resource.

8   Change the resource calendar for Ann Salinski. (Hint: Select Ann Salinski and then click the Resource Information button on the Standard toolbar.) Set November 25, 2002 as a nonworking day.

9   Assign resource MRB to subtasks of Market analysis; Ann Salinski to tasks in rows 15, 16, and 27; Jack Thomas to tasks in rows 20 and 21; Aileen MacElvoy to tasks in rows 20, 27, 29, and 30; Ron Timmons to the task in row 28; and Young & Young to the task in row 22.

10   Switch to the Cost table in Gantt Chart view. (Hint: Choose View, Table: Entry, Cost.)

11   Enter fixed costs as shown in Exhibit 4-4.

12   Save the project file as **My practice resources** without the baseline and close the project file.

	❶	Resource Name	Type	Material Label	Initials	Group	Max. Units	Std. Rate
1		Ann Salinski	Work		A	Finance	100%	$43.75/hr
2		Jack Thomas	Work		J	Sales	100%	$50.00/hr
3		Susan Gianni	Work		S	Business consultant	100%	$100.00/hr
4		Aileen MacElvoy	Work		A	Marketing	100%	$50.00/hr
5		Ron Timmons	Work		R	Marketing	100%	$48.00/hr
6		Solena Hernandez	Work		S	Market Analyst	100%	$0.00/hr
7		Young & Young	Work		Y	Advertising company	100%	$0.00/hr
8		MRB	Work		M	Market Research agency	100%	$0.00/hr

Exhibit 4-3: The Resource Sheet view after Step 7 of the Independent practice activity

	Task Name	Fixed Cost	Fixed Cost Accrual	Total Cost
10	⊟ **Market analysis**	**$0.00**	**Prorated**	**$18,000.00**
11	Survey through mail	$4,500.00	Prorated	$4,500.00
12	Survey through Web	$3,500.00	Prorated	$3,500.00
13	Purchase market dat	$10,000.00	Prorated	$10,000.00
14	⊟ **Finance**	**$0.00**	**Prorated**	**$1,750.00**
15	Determine budget	$0.00	Prorated	$1,050.00
16	Plan a strategy	$0.00	Prorated	$700.00
17	Get an approval	$0.00	Prorated	$0.00
18	⊟ **Marketing & sales**	**$0.00**	**Prorated**	**$35,127.00**
19	Pricing	$0.00	Prorated	$0.00
20	Sales recruitment	$0.00	Prorated	$800.00
21	Sales training	$0.00	Prorated	$400.00
22	⊟ **Advertise**	**$0.00**	**Prorated**	**$30,000.00**
23	Through television	$16,000.00	Prorated	$16,000.00
24	Through Web	$8,000.00	Prorated	$8,000.00
25	Through direct m:	$6,000.00	Prorated	$6,000.00
26	⊟ **Distribution**	**$0.00**	**Prorated**	**$3,927.00**

Exhibit 4-4: The Fixed cost details in the Cost table after Step 11 of the Independent practice activity

Unit 5

Working with task views

Complete this unit, and you'll know how to:

A Examine and customize Calendar view.

B Customize Gantt Chart and Network Diagram views.

Topic A: Working in Calendar view

Explanation
To effectively plan and monitor your project, you might want to look at all the tasks ending in a specific week or review specific project information in a calendar format. Project 2000 provides a view in a calendar format that you can customize for your project needs.

Calendar view

You can use Calendar view when you want to view the tasks scheduled for a particular day, week, or month. The *Calendar view* displays task information in a calendar format. Each task in Calendar view is represented by a bar that spans across the days and weeks according to its schedule.

By default, Calendar view displays seven days and four weeks of the current month. You can also display five days instead of seven days of a week. To view other months, you use the Previous month and the Next month buttons, or use the vertical scroll bar. Calendar view displays blue-bordered bars to represent the tasks. You'll notice that the summary tasks are not available in the default view and the nonworking days are shaded in gray. Exhibit 5-1 shows the default Calendar view.

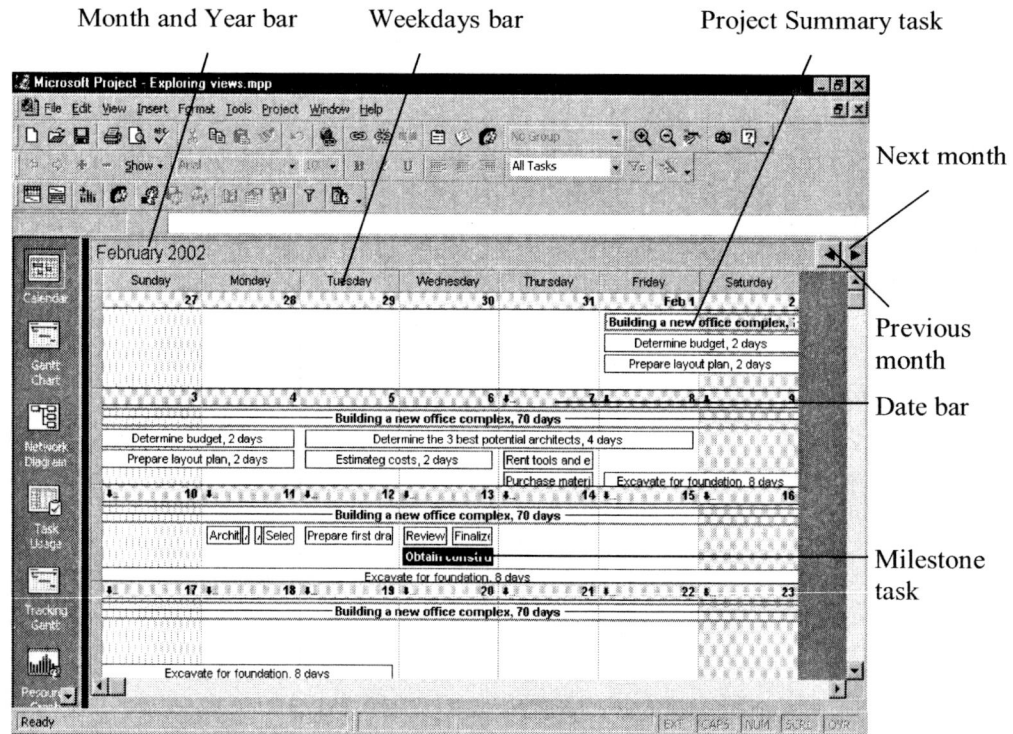

Exhibit 5-1: The Calendar view

You switch to Calendar view by choosing View, Calendar or by clicking the Calendar button on the View bar.

Do it!

A-1:   Exploring Calendar view

Here's how	Here's why
1 Open Exploring views	You'll explore Calendar view to examine the default settings.
2 Click [icon]	(The Calendar button is on the View bar.) To switch to Calendar view.
3 Observe the Month and Year bar	It displays the month and the year for which the project is scheduled.
4 Observe the Weekdays bar	By default, Project 2000 displays seven days of the week.
5 Observe the tasks	Notice that all tasks span across the days or weeks according to their schedule.
Observe the Project Summary task	This bar appears for each week throughout the life cycle of the project.
6 Observe the Milestone tasks	The milestone tasks appear as black bars.
7 Observe the vertical scroll bar	You can scroll to view the tasks scheduled for other weeks and months.

Customizing Calendar view

Explanation

You can customize Calendar view to display project information in a format that meets the needs of your project. For example, you can change the shading for all nonworking and working days of the project. You can also add information that does not appear in the default Calendar view. For example, you can include summary tasks, which are not displayed in the default view, if you want to see them on the project calendar. After you include the summary tasks, you might need to expand the Date bar to view them.

The other ways to customize your project in Calendar view include:

- Format the text within the task bars to distinguish one type of information from another.
- Change the horizontal and vertical lines that separate the calendar into weeks and days.
- Change the height of the week rows.
- Format the *timescale*. The timescale displays the time period.
- Format the date boxes to change their default color and size.
- Format the bar styles and bar patterns.

When you save your project file, the customized Calendar view is saved with it.

Do it!   **A-2: Customizing a project in Calendar view**

Here's how	Here's why
1 In the February 2002 calendar, select **Feb 1**	You'll customize the Calendar view.
2 Choose **Format, Bar Styles...**	To open the Bar Styles dialog box.
3 From the Task type list, select **Summary**	You'll add summary-task information to Calendar view.
4 Under Bar shape, from the Bar type list, select **Bar**	To represent summary tasks by bars.
From the Pattern list, select the option as shown	

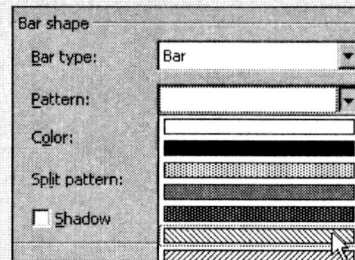

Here's how	Here's why
From the Color list, select **Red**	To add a red color to the bar.
Observe the Sample box	It displays a sample of the bar.
5 Click **OK**	To apply the settings.
6 Point to the Date bar	The pointer changes to a two-way arrow.
Drag the bar down as shown	

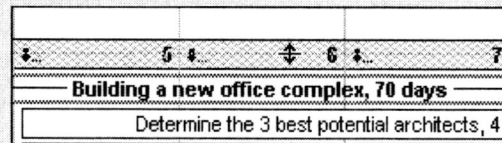

To view the summary tasks.

Observe the summary task bars

The summary bars appear with the pattern in red.

7	Choose **Format**, **Timescale…**	To open the Timescale dialog box.
8	Click the **Date Shading** tab	To display the options in it.
9	In the Show working time for list, verify that Outlander Spices construction (Project Calendar) is selected	You'll format this base calendar.
	Under Exception shading, in the Exception type list, verify that Base Calendar Working Days is selected	You'll add shading to the base calendar working days.
	From the Color list, select **Silver**	To add a silver shade to the working days of the base calendar.
10	Under Exception Shading, from the Exception type list, select **Base Calendar Nonworking Days**	You'll add different shading to the nonworking days.
	From the Color list, select **Yellow**	To add a yellow shade to the nonworking days of the base calendar.
11	Click **OK**	To apply the settings.
	Observe the calendar	Monday to Friday, the default working days are silver, and Saturday, Sunday, and the other nonworking days are yellow.
12	Save the project file as **My exploring views**	Save without the baseline if the Planning Wizard appears.

Topic B: Customizing other views

Explanation   In Project 2000, the most commonly used views are Gantt Chart and Network Diagram. You can customize these views to display information that meets your specific project needs.

Customizing Gantt Chart view

You use Gantt Chart view to enter task-related details. If you work in Gantt Chart view frequently, you might want to see specific task information on the Gantt Chart. For example, you can display task dates next to the task bar in the Gantt chart. This helps you to view both the start and finish dates of each task simultaneously instead of scrolling up to view the timescale.

You can also use the Gantt Chart Wizard to customize your working environment based on your project needs. This helps you format the Gantt chart quickly. You use the Gantt Chart Wizard by clicking the GanttChartWizard button on the Standard toolbar.

The wizard provides five formats – Standard, Critical path, Baseline, Other, and Custom chart. You can change the formats of the Gantt chart bars. For example, you can customize the Standard format of Gantt Chart view to display the task information with resources and dates, only resources, or only dates. You can also customize the view by hiding the link lines in the Gantt chart.

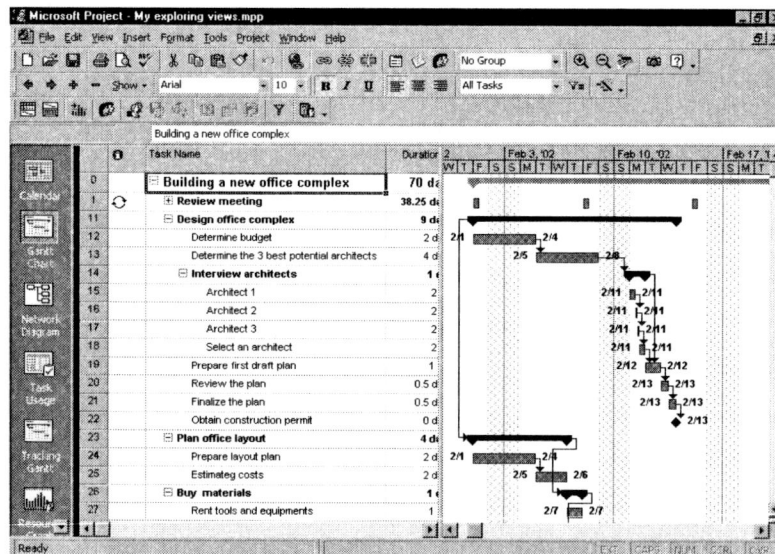

Exhibit 5-2: A sample customized Gantt Chart view

Do it!   **B-1:   Using the Gantt Chart Wizard**

Here's how	Here's why
1 Switch to Gantt Chart view	
2 Double-click **Task Name**	(The second field heading in the Gantt table.) The Column Definition dialog box appears.
3 Click **Best Fit**	To expand the column width to fit the complete text.
Observe the Gantt table	The column width increases and now the complete text is visible.
4 Click	(The GanttChartWizard button is on the Formatting toolbar.) To customize the Gantt chart by using the Gantt Chart Wizard.
5 Observe the first screen of the wizard	It displays the Gantt Chart Wizard welcome page.
Click **Next**	To move to the next screen of the wizard.
6 Verify that Standard is selected	By default, Project 2000 provides the Standard information in the Gantt chart.
Click **Next**	To move to the next screen.
7 Select **Dates**	You'll display the specific dates of the tasks in the Gantt chart.
Click **Next**	
8 Verify that Yes, please is selected	To display the links between dependent tasks.
Click **Next**	
9 Click **Format It**	To format the Gantt chart.
Click **Exit Wizard**	To exit the Gantt Chart Wizard after completing the format.
10 Observe the Gantt chart	All tasks now show the specific start and finish dates, which makes it easy to review the project (as shown in Exhibit 5-2).
Update the project file	

Customizing Network Diagram view

Explanation

You can customize Network Diagram view so that items on the network diagram stand out and make it easier to review and evaluate a project's progress. For example, you can change the color of summary tasks. Changing the color of the summary task boxes makes them easier to identify on the network diagram.

You can change the default information within the boxes. You can also enhance the appearance of the boxes or change border styles of the boxes. To do this, you use the Box Styles dialog box by choosing Format, Box Styles.

Do it!

B-2:   Customizing a project in Network Diagram view

Here's how	Here's why
1 Switch to Network Diagram view	
2 Choose **Format, Box Styles...**	To open the Box Styles dialog box. You'll format the network diagram boxes.
3 From the Style settings for list, verify that Project Summary is selected	You'll change the border color for it.
4 Under Border, from the Color list, select **Yellow**	To add a yellow border for the project summary task.
5 From the Style settings for list, select **Critical Summary**	You'll change the border style for it.
6 Under Border, from the Shape list, select the option as shown	

	To apply this style for all critical summary tasks.
7 Under Border, clear **Show horizontal gridlines**	To hide the horizontal gridlines in the task boxes.
Click **OK**	To apply the settings.
8 Observe the network diagram	Project 2000 formats the project summary tasks with a yellow border and changes the shape of the critical summary tasks. The horizontal gridlines are hidden for all critical summary tasks.
Click	(The Zoom Out button is on the Standard toolbar.) To zoom out so that you can view more nodes.
9 Update and close the project file	

Unit Summary: Working with task views

Topic A In this unit, you explored **Calendar view** by examining its components. Then you learned to **customize** this view by using the **Format** menu commands.

Topic B Next, you learned to **customize** Gantt Chart view by using the **Gantt Chart Wizard**. You also learned to **customize** Network Diagram view by using the options in the **Bar Styles** dialog box.

Independent practice activity

1 Open **Practice views**.

2 Switch to Calendar view.

3 Open the Timescale dialog box. (Hint: Choose Format, Timescale.)

4 Format the Daily titles to be Sun, Mon, Tue. (Hint: Click the Week Headings tab, if necessary. From the Daily titles list, select Sun, Mon, Tue.)

5 Under Top row, from the Pattern list, select a pattern. From the Color list, select a color. (Hint: Click the Date Boxes tab.)

6 Switch to Gantt Chart view.

7 Open the Gantt Chart Wizard. (Hint: Click the GanttChartWizard button.)

8 Select the Standard format and display information on the resources. Display the link lines and format the Gantt Chart view. (Hint: Click Next after selecting each option in the screens.)

9 Observe the task bars in the Gantt Chart pane. (Resource names appear and dates are not available.)

10 Switch to Network Diagram view.

11 Change the border color of the project summary task to black. (Hint: Choose Format, Box Styles.)

12 Observe the view. (Hint: Use the Zoom Out button, if necessary.)

13 Save as **My practice views** without a baseline, and close the project file.

Unit 6
Finalizing the task plan

Complete this unit, and you'll know how to:

A Edit task constraints and effort-driven scheduling to fine-tune your project.

B Resolve resource conflicts by identifying and adjusting resource overallocation.

Topic A: Finalizing the schedule

Explanation

After you've scheduled the tasks, you need to review them to see if they meet the project objectives. You must review your schedule and modify it early in the planning process so that the project runs effectively in its next phase. After you have reviewed your plan, you can fine-tune the schedule to meet the project deadline.

Editing task constraints

Task constraints such as Must Finish On, Finish No Later Than, and Must Start On often restrict Project 2000's capability to schedule all of a project's tasks. As a result, you might have to edit some of the task constraints to avoid conflicts in the schedule.

When you schedule your project to start from a fixed start date, Project 2000 pushes the schedule toward later dates to accommodate all the linked tasks. As a result, you might have to edit some task constraints to prevent Project 2000 from scheduling tasks to later dates. This helps you control the finish dates for your project. For example, the task Build the foundation has a Finish No Later Than constraint assigned to it. This constraint assigns a fixed finish date. You can reschedule it by imposing a constraint on the start date instead so that the start date is fixed, and Project 2000 schedules the task to start earlier.

Do it!

A-1: Editing a task constraint

Here's how	Here's why
1 Open Finalizing	You'll edit a task constraint in this project.
2 Select **Build the foundation**	(In row 31.)
Observe the task	The task Build the foundation starts on 2/15/02 and finishes on 3/5/02.
3 Click	To view the task bar.
Observe the link line	Both the tasks are scheduled based on the specified constraint.
4 Click	To open the Task Information dialog box.
5 Verify that the Advanced tab is active	To display the options in it.

6	Under Constrain task, in the Constraint type list, observe that Finish No Later Than is selected	This is the constraint assigned to this task that you'll edit.
	From the Constraint type list, select **Start No Later Than**	This is the new constraint for the task.
	In the Constraint date box, enter **2/13/2002**	This will be the new start date.
7	Click **OK**	To apply the changes. The Planning Wizard dialog box opens.
	Select the option shown	

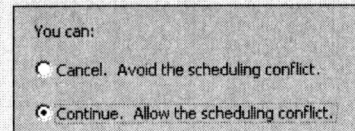

> You can:
>
> ○ Cancel. Avoid the scheduling conflict.
>
> ⦿ Continue. Allow the scheduling conflict.

	Click **OK**	
8	Point as shown	

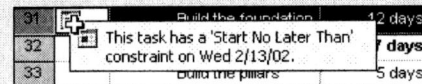

> | 31 | | Build the foundation | 12 days |
> | 32 | | ⬚ This task has a 'Start No Later Than' constraint on Wed 2/13/02. | days |
> | 33 | | Build the pillars | 5 days |

		The ScreenTip describes the new constraint.
	Observe the Start and Finish date fields	Project 2000 automatically shifts the finish date based on the start date and duration.
	Deselect the row	Click any other cell.
9	Save the project file as **My finalizing**	

Effort-driven schedules

Explanation

When you add or remove resources from a task, Project 2000 modifies the duration of the task to utilize the additional, or fewer resources, but does not change the total effort for the task. This is called *effort-driven scheduling.* By default, Project 2000 uses effort-driven scheduling to allocate resources.

Consider a task in which the duration of work is 4 days, and 2 resources are assigned to it for 8 hours a day. Total effort is duration multiplied by resources. The *total effort* on this task is 64 hours (8 hours multiplied by 4 days multiplied by 2 resources). If you add 2 additional resources to this task, Project 2000 decreases the task duration to two days, keeping the total effort constant.

When you edit the effort-driven schedule, Project 2000 modifies only the total effort for the task without affecting the task duration. In this way, you can keep the total duration of your project in control without extending the finish date.

Editing an effort-driven schedule

You can edit the effort-driven schedule only for fixed-duration or fixed-unit types of tasks, because their duration is constant. Disabling effort-driven scheduling for a fixed-duration type of task helps you determine the effect of adding or removing a resource on the total amount of work involved in a task. For example, to ensure that the task Plan office layout is not delayed, you can assign two more resources to its subtasks. Since the subtasks Prepare layout plan and Estimate costs are of fixed-unit type, you have to first edit their effort-driven scheduling. When you clear Effort driven for the subtasks of Plan office layout, Project 2000 automatically changes the total effort on this task and keeps the duration of the tasks unchanged.

To edit the effort-driven schedule:

1   Select the task whose effort-driven schedule you want to modify.
2   Click the Task Information button to open the Task Information dialog box.
3   Click the Advanced tab.
4   Clear Effort driven to modify the total work on a task while keeping the duration unchanged.

Do it!

A-2:   Editing an effort-driven schedule

Here's how	Here's why
1 In row 27, observe the Duration field	The task is scheduled for 1 day.
2 Double-click **Rent tools and equipment**	(In row 27.) You will assign a new resource, but will not clear the effort-driven setting.
Verify that the Advanced tab is active	
Verify that Effort driven is checked	You'll observe the changes that Project 2000 makes to the task duration when Effort driven is checked.
3 Click the **Resources** tab	To assign a resource.
In the Resource Name field, select the second cell	To activate it. A drop-down arrow appears in the cell.
Click the drop-down arrow	To display the list of resources available for the project.
Select **Fred**	This will be the new resource.
Click **OK**	
Observe the Duration field	The duration for this task reduces to 0.5 days after the new resource is added to it.

4	Double-click **Estimate costs**	(In row 25.) To assign a resource to it.
5	Verify that the Resources tab is active	
	From the Resources list, select **Jack Thomas**	(Click the second cell and select Jack Thomas from the drop-down list.) To add a resource for this task.
6	Click the **Advanced** tab	You'll clear Effort driven for this task to keep the duration of the task constant.
	Clear **Effort driven**	
7	Click **OK**	To close the dialog box.
	Observe the duration	Project 2000 keeps the duration fixed, as it is not an effort-driven task.
8	Update the project file	

Topic B: Resolving resource conflicts

Explanation

After resources are assigned to tasks, you might want to view the resource workloads to analyze resource utilization. If you have assigned a single resource for different tasks, the resource might exceed its capacity. Project 2000 calculates and marks these resources as overallocated resources. You can resolve overallocation by leveling resources.

Resource overallocation

Resources are *overallocated* when they are scheduled to do more work than can be accomplished in the specified time. Project 2000 identifies resources as being overallocated when the sum of units assigned to all tasks exceeds the number of units defined in the MaxUnits field.

Identifying resource overallocation

You can easily identify resources that are overallocated because information regarding resource overallocation is in red by default. Project 2000 provides different views that display the nature of resource allocation in your project. Resource Sheet view displays the relevant information for overallocated resources. Resource Graph view displays a graphical representation of the workload of a single resource. Resource Usage view displays information about the resources such as their allocation, overallocation of cost, and work.

To display information on resource overallocation in Resource Usage view, you must first add the Overallocation field to the view. When you add this field, Resource Usage view displays overallocation details for a resource, like the number of overallocated hours for a particular day as shown in Exhibit 6-1.

To add the Overallocation field:

1   Switch to Resource Usage view.
2   Choose Format, Detail Styles to open the Detail Styles dialog box.
3   From the Available fields list, select Overallocation.
4   Click Show to include the selected field in the Show these fields list.
5   Click OK.

Overallocation indicator   Overallocation field   Number of Overallocated hours

	Resource Name	Work	Details	T	F	S	S	M	T	W
	⊞ Unassigned	0 hrs	Work							
			Overall							
1	⊟ Kathy Sinclair	60 hrs	Work		16h	11h		10.5h	8h	8
	This resource should be leveled based on a Day by Day setting.		Overall		8h	5.5h		2.5h		
			Work		8h	5.5h		2.5h		
			Overall							
	Determine the b	32 hrs	Work		8h	5.5h		8h	8h	2.5
			Overall							
	Interview archite	8 hrs	Work							5.5
			Overall							
	Finalize the plar	4 hrs	Work							
			Overall							
2	⊟ Jack Thomas	37.5 hrs	Work		8h	5.5h	2.5h	5.5h	8h	8
			Overall							
	Interview archite	5.5 hrs	Work							5.5
			Overall							
	Prepare layout p	16 hrs	Work		8h	5.5h	2.5h			
			Overall							
	Estimate costs	16 hrs	Work					5.5h	8h	2.5
			Overall							
3	⊟ Curt Allen	2 hrs	Work							2

Exhibit 6-1: The Resource Usage view

Do it!

B-1: Identifying resource overallocation

Here's how	Here's why
1 Click [icon]	(The Resource Usage button is on the View bar.) To switch to the Resource Usage view and add the Overallocation field to this view.
2 Observe Kathy Sinclair	You can see the tasks assigned to this resource. The Overallocation field is not available for this resource.
3 Choose **Format, Detail Styles...**	To open the Detail Styles dialog box.
Verify that the Usage Details tab is active	
4 From the Available fields list, select **Overallocation**	You'll add this field in the Resource Usage view.
5 Click **Show**	To include the selected field in the Show these fields list.
Observe the Show these fields list	The Overallocation field is included in the list.
6 Click **OK**	To apply the settings.

7	Select **Kathy Sinclair**	You'll review the overallocated hours for this resource.
	Click ⟨icon⟩	To view the Overallocation field.
8	Observe the Resource Usage view	(Scroll horizontally, if necessary.) The overallocated resources are in red, and it also shows the number of overallocated hours for the resource (as shown in Exhibit 6-1).
	Point to the indicator icon next to Kathy Sinclair	A ScreenTip appears that prompts you to level the resource.
9	Update the project file	

Resolving resource overallocation

Explanation

After you have identified resources that are overallocated, you can level the resources. Resolving resource overallocation often depends on the limitations of the project. These limitations might include the project budget, resource availability, and the flexibility within the tasks that make up the schedule.

Resource leveling

Resource leveling is the process of resolving resource overallocation by adjusting resource assignment for a project. You can level resources by using the automatic leveling feature of Project 2000 or by manually leveling them. However, when you use the automatic feature of Project 2000 to level overallocated resources, the task becomes delayed until the resources are available. This could push the finish date of the project beyond your plan. In addition, the automatic resource-leveling feature has other limitations. For example, you might want to reduce the workload on an overallocated resource by assigning some of its tasks to an underallocated resource. When this occurs, you cannot use automatic resource leveling, as it doesn't reassign resources automatically.

To overcome the limitations of automatic leveling by Project 2000, you can level resources manually in any of the following ways:

- Replace the overallocated resource with an underallocated resource.
- Assign an additional resource to the task.
- Reduce the work assignments of a task and increase the duration for its completion.
- Increase the working time of the resource.

You can use Resource Allocation view to replace resources by clicking the Resource Allocation View button on the Resource Management toolbar. Exhibit 6-2 displays the resource overallocation in Resource Allocation view.

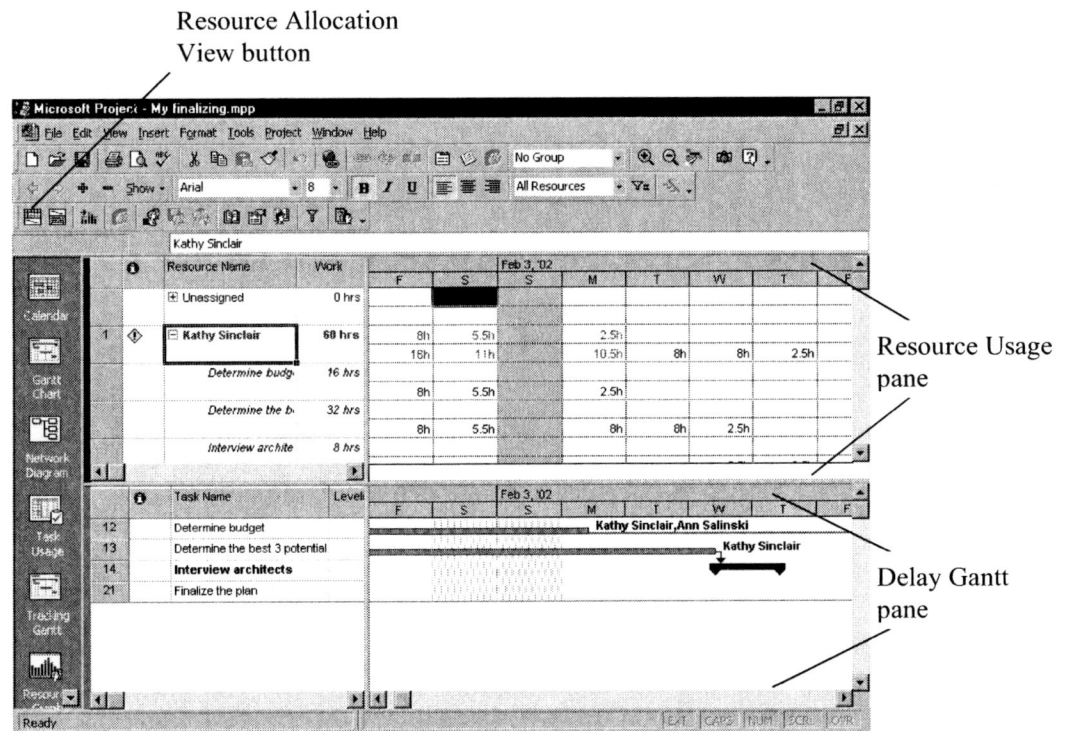

Exhibit 6-2: The Resource Allocation view

Do it!

B-2: Adjusting resource leveling manually

Here's how	Here's why
1 Switch to Resource Sheet view	
2 Observe the view	Kathy Sinclair is in red, indicating that she is an overallocated resource.
3 Switch to Gantt Chart view	You'll replace resources for the task with an overallocated resource to level the resources.
4 Choose **View, Toolbars, Resource Management**	To display the Resource Management toolbar. It appears below the Formatting toolbar.
5 Click ▣	The Resource Allocation View button is on the Resource Management toolbar.
Observe the view	The Resource Allocation view shows the Resource Usage view in the upper pane and the Delay Gantt view in the lower pane.
Select **Kathy Sinclair**	To view all the tasks assigned to her (as shown in Exhibit 6-2).
Observe the lower pane	It shows all the tasks of the overallocated resource, Kathy.

6	In the Delay Gantt pane, select **Determine budget**	(The lower pane.) You'll replace the resource for this task.
7	Click	To open the Assign Resources dialog box.
	In the Name list, verify that Kathy Sinclair is selected	You'll replace this resource.
8	Click **Replace**	
	Observe the dialog box	It prompts for a replacement of the selected resource with another.
	From the Name list, select **Susan Gianni**	You'll replace Kathy Sinclair with Susan Gianni.
	Click **OK**	To replace the overallocated resource.
9	Click **Close**	To close the dialog box.
	Deselect the cell	
10	Observe the Delay Gantt pane	You'll see that the task is no longer available in it because it is no longer assigned to Kathy.
	Observe the Resource Usage pane	Kathy Sinclair is not in red, as she is no longer overallocated.
11	Update and close the project file	

Unit Summary: Finalizing the task plan

Topic A   In this unit, you learned to fine-tune your project by editing **task constraints** and the **effort-driven schedule** by using the **Task Information** dialog box.

Topic B   Next, you learned to resolve resource conflicts by first **identifying** resource overallocation, and then **manually leveling** them by replacing resources. You used the **Resource Allocation view** to review and resolve resource overalloction.

Independent practice activity

1   Open **Practice finalize**.

2   Edit the task constraint on task '**Sales training**' to Finish No Later Than. Edit the constraint date to 10/10/02.

3   Observe the resources assigned to the task 'Determine budget.'

4   Assign another resource to '**Determine budget**' and clear Effort driven for this task.

5   Observe that the duration of the task remains the same.

6   Switch to Resource Usage view.

7   Observe the resource overallocation.

8   Include the Overallocation field. (Hint: Choose Format, Detail Styles and then add the Overallocation field.)

9   Switch to Gantt Chart view. Switch to Resource Allocation view. (Hint: In Gantt Chart view, click the Resource Allocation View button.)

10 Level Jack Thomas by replacing him with Ron Timmons for the task Pricing. (Hint: Select Pricing in the Delay Gantt pane, and click the Assign Resources button.)

11 Save as **My practice finalize** without a baseline, and close the project file.

U n i t   7

Filtering, grouping, and sorting

Complete this unit, and you'll know how to:

A Use standard filters and AutoFilters to view data and create an interactive filter.

B Use predefined groups and create a custom group.

C Sort data in a project file to manipulate the task and resource views.

Topic A: Working with filters

Explanation

As a project manager, you often need to concentrate on a specific set of tasks or resources. For example, you may want to view the costs for a specific consultant or review only the critical tasks. *Filters* allow you to view only those tasks and resources that meet specified criteria.

Filtering tasks and resources

Project 2000 provides several *standard filters*. The two types of standard filters that display specific information are *Task filters* and *Resource filters*. The Task filters selectively display tasks. By default, the All Tasks filter is applied to task views such as Calendar, Gantt Chart, Task Usage, Network Diagram, and Tracking Gantt. The Resource filters selectively display resources and the All Resources filter is applied by default to all resource views, such as Resource Graph, Resource Sheet, and Resource Usage.

You can use the standard filters either for tasks or resources. For example, in a task view, you might want to see tasks that end within a specified time frame. In this case, you apply the Date Range filter to the complete task list. When you apply a filter to the task list, Project 2000 does not delete information from your project—it simply hides it from view. You can apply a filter by choosing Project, Filtered for. A submenu consisting of a list of filter options appears.

You can also apply standard filters by clicking the drop-down arrow in the Filter box in the Formatting toolbar and then selecting a filter from it.

Do it!

A-1: Using a standard filter

Here's how	Here's why
1 Open Filtering	You'll filter tasks by using a standard filter in the Gantt Chart.
2 Observe the task list	The complete task list appears.
3 Choose **Project, Filtered for: All Tasks, Date Range...**	To view the tasks between March and May 2002. The Date Range dialog box appears.
4 Enter the start date shown	
Click **OK**	The Date Range dialog box appears.

Enter the finish date shown

Date Range	? X
And before:	OK
5/1/02	Cancel

Click **OK**

5   Observe the task list

The tasks that fall within the specified date range appear.

6   Save the project file as **My filtering**

AutoFilters

Explanation

In addition to the standard filters, Project 2000 also provides *AutoFilters*. AutoFilters are a combination of Project 2000 filters and are designed to be performed on the task and resource list of the current view that you're working with. When you have applied a standard filter to the task list, and want to view information within a particular field in the Gantt table, the AutoFilter option in Project 2000 helps filter this information. For example, after applying the Date Range filter to display only the tasks for the specified date range, you might want to see tasks that will take more than a week to complete. To do this, you can apply an AutoFilter to the Duration field.

You use AutoFilter by choosing Project, Filtered for, AutoFilter. When you select this option, the AutoFilter button on the Formatting toolbar is selected. You'll also see that a drop-down menu is added to each field heading. You apply an AutoFilter to a field by clicking the drop-down arrow and selecting a filter. After you have applied an AutoFilter, you can turn off the AutoFilter by clicking the AutoFilter button to return to the previous list.

Do it!

A-2:   Using an AutoFilter

Here's how	Here's why
1 Choose **Project, Filtered for: Date Range..., AutoFilter**	You'll apply an AutoFilter to filter a field.
Observe the fields	A drop-down arrow appears in each field heading.
Observe the AutoFilter button	(On the Formatting toolbar.) The button is selected, indicating that the AutoFilter is on.
2 In the Duration field, click the drop-down arrow	To display the list of filters available for this field.
Select **> 1 week**	To filter the field based on this condition.
3 Observe the Duration field	The field heading appears in blue. The tasks are filtered and the field displays only those tasks that take more than 7 days.

4 Click ▼=	To turn off the AutoFilter option. The drop-down arrows are no longer available.
Choose **Project, Filtered for: Date Range..., All Tasks**	To view the complete task list.
5 Update the project file	

Interactive filters

Explanation

You can create your own *interactive filters* to selectively view your task or resource list. An interactive filter displays a dialog box that allows you to enter different filter criteria each time you apply the filter. You need to create an interactive filter when the predefined filters in Project 2000 do not provide the information you need. For example, you might want to filter the tasks or resources with different cost values. The predefined standard cost filters in Project 2000 allow you to enter only one cost value at a time. You can apply an interactive filter to tasks or resources to view the result with different values every time you filter them. However, to filter costs for tasks or resources, you have to switch to the Cost table within the respective view. When you switch to the Cost table, the column headings of the resource sheet change. The sheet provides information such as Cost, Baseline Cost, Variance, Actual Cost, and Remaining. Because you're not saving the project file with a baseline, there is no data in this field. You'll see the same cost figure in the Cost, Variance, and Remaining fields.

To create an interactive filter:

1   Choose Project, Filtered for, More Filters to open the More Filters dialog box.
2   Click New to create a new custom filter. The Filter Definition dialog box appears.
3   In the Name box, specify a name for the filter.
4   Check Show in menu to include the interactive filter in the list of other filters.
5   In the Field name, select the first cell. The cell displays a drop-down list. Select a field name from the list.
6   In the Test field, select a test from the list.
7   In the Value(s) field, specify a message within quotation marks followed by a question mark.
8   Click OK to close the Filter Definition dialog box.
9   Click Apply to use the filter or click Close to use the filter later.

Do it!   **A-3:   Creating an interactive filter**

Here's how	Here's why
1 Switch to Resource Sheet view	
2 Choose **View, Table: Entry, Cost**	To switch to the Cost table within Resource Sheet view.
Observe the Cost table	The column fields display cost-related information. Because Baseline Cost is not entered, the cost is the same in other fields.
3 Choose **Project, Filtered For: All Resources, More Filters...**	To open the More Filters dialog box.
4 Click **New**	To create an interactive filter. The Filter Definition in 'My filtering' dialog box appears.
5 Edit the Name box to read **Resource Cost**	This will be the name of your filter.
Check **Show in menu**	To add the interactive filter to the list of existing filters.
6 In the Field Name, select the first cell	It displays a drop-down list.
From the drop-down list, select **Cost**	(You may need to scroll.) To filter the task based on cost.
7 In the Test field, select the first cell	
From the drop-down list, select **is greater than**	This is the criteria on which you will filter.
8 In the Value(s) field, enter **"Cost greater than"?**	To specify the message.
9 Click **OK**	To go back to the More Filters dialog box.
Verify that Resource Cost is selected in the list	
Click **Apply**	To apply and open the filter dialog box.

10 Observe the dialog box

Resource Cost	? ✕
Cost greater than	OK
	Cancel

Project 2000 creates an interactive filter dialog box called Resource Cost and displays the message "Cost greater than."

In the Cost greater than box, enter **250**

By default, Microsoft Project 2000 assigns a dollar sign ($) to the value entered.

Click **OK**

To filter the list based on the specified value.

11 Observe the table

Only 5 resources that have a cost of over $250 appear in the list.

12 Update the project file

Topic B: Working with groups

Explanation

You can group tasks or resources in a view by choosing criteria to organize the information without changing the actual structure of your project. For example, you might want to group the tasks based on their duration. Project 2000 provides the Group by feature to group the tasks and resources that meet specified criteria.

Grouping tasks and resources

Project 2000 provides two types of predefined groups, *task groups* and *resource groups*. You can apply the task groups to task sheet views, such as Gantt Chart, Task Usage, and Tracking Gantt view. The resource groups can be applied only to resource sheet views such as Resource Sheet, Resource Usage, and Resource Allocation views. You cannot apply any grouping to Calendar, Network Diagram, and Resources Graph views. You apply groups by choosing Project, Group by. A submenu consisting of a list of groups appears.

You can also apply groups by clicking the drop-down arrow in the Group By box in the Standard toolbar and then selecting a group from it.

Do it!

B-1: Using a predefined group

Here's how	Here's why
1 Switch to Gantt Chart view	You'll group tasks by using a predefined group in the Gantt Chart.
2 Observe the task list	The complete task list appears.
3 Choose **Project, Group by: No Group, Duration**	To group the tasks based on their duration.
4 Observe the Gantt table	The tasks are grouped based on their duration.
5 Choose **Project, Group by: Duration, No Group**	To view the complete task list without grouping.
6 Update the project file	

Creating custom groups

Explanation

You can create a custom group to selectively group tasks and resources when the predefined groups don't return the required information.

To create a custom group:
1 Choose Project, Group by, More Groups to open the More Groups dialog box.
2 Click New to open the Group Definition dialog box.
3 In the Name box, specify a name for the group.
4 In the Field name, select the first cell. Select a field name from the list.

     5   In the Order field, select the first cell. Select an option from the list.

     6   Click Define Group Intervals to open the Define Group Interval dialog box.

     7   From the Group on list, select an option.

     8   Click OK to close the Define Group Interval dialog box.

     9   Click OK to close the Group Definition dialog box.

     10 Click Apply to group the task.

Do it!

B-2: Creating a custom group

Here's how	Here's why
1 Choose **Project**, **Group by: No Group**, **More Groups...**	To open the More Groups dialog box.
2 Click **New**	(To open the Group Definition dialog box.) You'll create a custom group.
3 Edit the Name box to read **Duration in weeks**	This will be the name of the custom group.
4 In the Field Name, select the first cell	It displays a drop-down list.
From the drop-down list, select **Duration**	(You may need to scroll.) To group the tasks based on their duration.
5 In the Order field, select the first cell	
From the drop-down list, select **Descending**	You'll group the tasks in descending order.
6 Click **Define Group Intervals**	To open the Define Group Interval dialog box.
From the Group on list, select **Weeks**	You'll group the tasks based on duration in weeks.
7 Click **OK**	To close the Define Group Interval dialog box.
8 Click **OK**	To close the Group Definition dialog box.

9	Verify that **Duration in weeks** is selected in the list	
10	Click **Apply**	To apply the custom group.
11	Observe the Gantt chart table	Project 2000 groups all the tasks based on their duration in weeks.
12	Choose **Project, Group by: Duration in weeks, No Group**	To view the tasks without grouping.
13	Update the project file	

Topic C: Sorting a view

Explanation

You can *sort* tasks and resources by criteria, such as task name, deadline, and resource name. Sorting produces a display of tasks and resources in a specified sequence.

Sorting tasks

During the planning process, you might want to view tasks sorted by start date or finish date to easily read and analyze the task list. Sorting tasks, however, does not alter the task ID numbers. So, you can restore the task list to its original order by sorting the tasks by their ID. By default, Project 2000 sorts tasks in ascending order.

You sort tasks by choosing Project, Sort. A submenu consisting of a list of sort options appears. You can then select an option to sort the task list.

Do it!

C-1:   Sorting tasks

Here's how	Here's why
1 Observe the tasks in row 11 and 23	The task Design office complex in row 11 and Plan office layout in row 23 start on the same date but finish on different dates. You'll view the task list sorted on finish dates.
2 Choose **Project, Sort, by Finish Date**	To sort the task list according to the finish dates. By default, Project 2000 sorts tasks in ascending order.
3 Observe the task list	The task Plan office layout appears before Design office complex because it finishes earlier.
4 Update the project file	

Sorting resources

Explanation

You might also want to sort resources or view them in a specific sequence. For example, you might want to view all resources in alphabetical order. To sort a resource list, you have to switch to Resource Sheet view. You can sort resources based on criteria such as group, name, priority, and cost.

You can also use more than one sort criteria. For example, you can sort resources first alphabetically according to their group and then, sort the grouped resources by their names. Exhibit 7-1 shows the resources that are sorted first, by group and then by name. However, to sort resources based on cost, you have to switch to the Cost table by choosing View, Table, Cost.

	ⓘ	Resource Name	Type	Material Label	Initials	Group
6		Susan Gianni	Work		S	Business consultant
3		Curt Allen	Work		C	External
8		Fred	Work		F	External
7		Joe Simmons	Work		J	External
5		Ann Salinski	Work		A	Finance
4		Eric	Work		E	Finance
12		Sprinkler	Work		S	Hired equipment
10		Jerry	Work		J	Labor
11		Laurie Macurthy	Work		L	Labor
9		Tim Walson	Work		T	Labor
2		Jack Thomas	Work		J	Planner
14		Wood	Material	cubic feet	W	Purchased
13		Paint	Material	gallon	P	Purchased
1		Kathy Sinclair	Work		K	Review

Exhibit 7-1: A sample of a sorted resource sheet

Do it!

C-2:   Sorting resources

Here's how	Here's why
1 Switch to Resource Sheet view	You'll sort resources based on specific criteria.
2 Switch to the Entry table	(Choose View, Table: Cost, Entry.) You'll use the column headings to create the sort order.
3 Choose **Project**, **Sort**, **Sort by...**	To open the Sort dialog box. You'll sort resources by specifying more than one criterion.
Verify that Permanently renumber resources is cleared	By default, this option is clear so you can reorder the resources with their original ID after sorting.
4 From the Sort by list, select **Group**	This will be the first criterion for sorting resources.
5 From the Then by list, select **Name**	This will be the second sorting criterion.
6 Click **Sort**	To sort the resource names first by Group, and then, by Name.
Observe the resource sheet	You'll see that Project 2000 has sorted resources based on the specified criteria (as shown in Exhibit 7-1).
7 Update the project file	

Renumbering a sorted list

Sorting does not change the ID numbers of the tasks or resources. This might cause confusion because the sequencing is affected. To follow a sequenced order of tasks and resources in the project, you renumber the sorted list. When you renumber tasks and resources on their respective sheets, the original order of each sheet is changed. Exhibit 7-2 shows the resource list with their new ID numbers.

By default, the Permanently renumber option in the Sort dialog box is cleared. To renumber resources or tasks, you open the Sort dialog box and then check Permanently renumber resources or Permanently renumber tasks respectively. After you check this option, Project 2000 renumbers the sorted list.

	❶	Resource Name	Type	Material Label	Initials	Group
1		Susan Gianni	Work		S	Business consultant
2		Curt Allen	Work		C	External
3		Fred	Work		F	External
4		Joe Simmons	Work		J	External
5		Ann Salinski	Work		A	Finance
6		Eric	Work		E	Finance
7		Sprinkler	Work		S	Hired equipment
8		Jerry	Work		J	Labor
9		Laurie Macurthy	Work		L	Labor
10		Tim Walson	Work		T	Labor
11		Jack Thomas	Work		J	Planner
12		Wood	Material	cubic feet	W	Purchased
13		Paint	Material	gallon	P	Purchased
14		Kathy Sinclair	Work		K	Review

Exhibit 7-2: A sample of the renumbered sorted list

Do it!

C-3:   Renumbering the sorted resource list

Here's how	Here's why
1 Choose **Project**, **Sort**, **Sort by...**	To open the Sort dialog box. You'll renumber the sorted resource list.
2 Check **Permanently renumber resources**	☑ Permanently renumber resources
Click **Sort**	To establish a new order of resources.
3 Observe the ID field	The sorted resource list appears with new ID numbers (as shown in Exhibit 7-2).
4 Update and close the project file	

Unit Summary: Filtering, grouping, and sorting

Topic A   In this unit, you learned to apply **standard filters**. You also learned to apply **AutoFilter** to a specific field. Then, you learned to create a **custom** filter by using the **More Filters** dialog box.

Topic B   Next, you learned to apply **predefined groups**. You also learned to create a **custom** group.

Topic C   Finally, you learned to **sort the task** and **resource lists** by specifying criteria with the **Sort** command. You also learned to permanently renumber the sorted list by checking **Permanently renumber resources** in the **Sort** dialog box.

Independent practice activity

1 Open **Practice filter**.

2 Filter the task list to view the summary tasks by using the standard filter.

3 In the Duration field, use the AutoFilter to view the task that has a duration of 6 days.

4 Turn off the AutoFilter. (Hint: Click the AutoFilter button.)

5 Switch to Resource Sheet view. Filter resources to view those who belong to group Marketing. (Hint: Choose Project, Filtered for: All Resources, Group. Enter the group name.)

6 Observe the view.

7 Apply the All Resources filter to the view.

8 Sort the resources without permanently renumbering them, first by Group, and then by Name. (Hint: Clear Permanently renumber resources.)

9 Observe the view. Compare your result with the view in Exhibit 7-3.

10 Save as **My practice filter** without a baseline and close the project file.

	🛈	Resource Name	Type	Material Labe	Initials	Group	Max. Units	Std. Rate	Ovt. Rate	Cost/Use	Accrue
7		Young & Young	Work		Y	Advertising company	100%	$120.00/hr	$0.00/hr	$0.00	Prorated
3		Susan Gianni	Work		S	Business consultant	100%	$100.00/hr	$0.00/hr	$0.00	Prorated
1		Ann Salinski	Work		A	Finance	100%	$43.75/hr	$0.00/hr	$0.00	Prorated
6		Solena Hernandez	Work		S	Market Analyst	100%	$100.00/hr	$0.00/hr	$0.00	Prorated
8		MRB	Work		M	Market Research agency	100%	$120.00/hr	$0.00/hr	$0.00	Prorated
4		Aileen MacElvoy	Work		A	Marketing	100%	$50.00/hr	$0.00/hr	$0.00	Prorated
5		Ron Timmons	Work		R	Marketing	100%	$48.00/hr	$0.00/hr	$0.00	Prorated
2		Jack Thomas	Work		J	Sales	100%	$50.00/hr	$0.00/hr	$0.00	Prorated

Exhibit 7-3: The sorted resource list after Step 8 of the Independent practice activity

Project 2000: Basic

Course summary

This summary contains information to help you bring the course to a successful conclusion. Using this information, you will be able to:

A Use the summary text to reinforce what you've learned in class.

B Determine the next courses in this series (if any), as well as any other resources that might help you continue to learn about Project 2000.

Topic A: Course summary

Use the following summary text to reinforce what you've learned in class.

Project 2000: Basic

Unit 1

In this Unit, you learned the **concepts** of **project management**. You learned about the basic tasks required to plan a project, and how **Microsoft Project 2000** helps you to manage your project in an effective and efficient manner. Then, you learned to **start** Microsoft Project 2000 and **open** an existing file to **navigate** different views in Project 2000. Next, you learned to use the **Office Assistant**. You also learned to create a **new** project file and learned to **save** it by using the **Save As** command and by setting a default folder and **Auto Save**. Finally, you learned to **close** the active project file and **exit** Project 2000.

Unit 2

In this unit, you learned to **create** a **task list** by entering task details in the Gantt table. You learned to **modify** the **task list** and also to **move** a task from one position to another. You also learned to **arrange** tasks in an outline by building the **Work Breakdown Structure** and learned to **hide subtasks**. Next, you also learned to add a **recurring task** to the task list by using the **Recurring Task Information** dialog box. Finally, you learned to **view**, **define**, and apply **WBS codes**.

Unit 3

In this unit, you learned to **link** tasks by using the **Link Tasks** button and added **lead time** to tasks by using the **Task Dependency** dialog box. You also learned to **unlink** tasks. Then, you modified a task list while in Network Diagram view. Next, you learned to specify a **task type**, **milestone tasks**, and **task constraints** by using the **Task Information** dialog box.

Unit 4

In this unit, you learned to create a **base calendar**. You learned to create a **resource pool** and created a **resource calendar**. Next, you learned to **assign resources** to tasks by using the **Assign Resources** button. You also learned to create a **task calendar**. Next, you learned to work with **resource costs** and **assigned** a **fixed cost** by using the **Cost** table.

Unit 5

In this unit, you **explored** Calendar view by examining its components and learned to **customize** your project calendar in it by using the **Format** menu commands. Next, you learned to **customize** Gantt Chart view by using the **GanttChartWizard** button. You also learned to **customize** Network Diagram view by using the options in the **Bar Styles** dialog box.

Unit 6

In this unit, you learned to fine-tune your project by editing **task constraints** and the **effort-driven schedule**. Next, you learned to resolve resource conflicts by first **identifying** resource overallocation and then **manually leveling** them by replacing resources by using **Resource Allocation view**.

Unit 7

In this unit, you learned to apply **standard filters** and use the **AutoFilter**. Then, you learned to create an **interactive filter**. You also learned to apply **predefined groups** and create a **custom group**. Next, you learned to **sort** the **task list** and **resource list** by specifying a criterion with the **Sort** command. Finally, you learned to permanently renumber the sorted list by checking **Permanently renumber resources** in the **Sort** dialog box.

Topic B: Continued learning after class

It is impossible to learn to use any software effectively in a single day. To get the most out of this class, you should begin working with Project 2000 to perform real tasks as soon as possible. Course Technology also offers resources for continued learning.

Next courses in this series

This is the first course in this series. The next course in the series is:

- *Project 2000: Advanced*

Other resources

In addition to the other courses in this series, you might also find some of these Course Technology resources useful as you continue to learn about Project 2000. For more information, visit www.course.com.

- *Course CBT: Microsoft Project 2000 Introductory Concepts and Techniques ISBN: 0-7895-5963-3*

Project 2000: Basic

Quick reference

Button	Keystrokes	What It Does
		To display Calendar view.
		To display Gantt Chart view.
		To display Network Diagram view.
		To display Task Usage view.
		To display Tracking Gantt view.
		To display Resource Graph view.
		To display Resource Sheet view.
		To display Resource Usage view.
		To scroll down the View bar.
		To scroll up the View bar.
	CTRL +S	To save changes.
		To indent tasks.
		To outdent tasks.

🔗	CTRL + F2	To link tasks.
🐀		To go to the selected task in the Gantt chart pane.
🔗		To unlink tasks.
📋		To open the Task information dialog box.
👥	ALT + F10	To assign resources to tasks.
🪄		To open the GanttChartWizard.
🔍		To zoom out the view.
🔍		To zoom in the view.
📊		To display Resource Allocation view.
▽=		To turn off the AutoFilter option.

Index